Mary Page
Peter Guthrie
Sloan Sable

Rules of the Game 1

Grammar through
Discovery

EDUCATORS PUBLISHING SERVICE
Cambridge and Toronto

Printed in USA

ISBN 978-0-8388-2237-1

10 11 12 PPG 12 11 10

CONTENTS

CONTENTS

ACKNOWLEDGMENTS

We have long been intrigued with the idea of teaching grammar inductively. Now that we have had the chance to put our ideas on paper, we find that we have not completed the process by ourselves.

To the people behind the scenes who have made this book possible we give our thanks and appreciation:

Jane Knox for her advice and encouragement;
Sarah for her support and good humor;
Doug, Tad, and Scout for time and patience;
Bob, Alan, and Sarah for their encouragement and support; and
Our students for their thoughtful responses to an endless stream of grammar exercises.

INTRODUCTION

In *Rules of the Game* we set out to write a grammar book that would encourage students to discover that grammar is just another name for the patterns that exist in language. In our own teaching, we have discovered that students learn grammar more effectively if they can, in some sense, recreate the process by which rules and definitions have evolved. To achieve this goal, we start each lesson with examples and directed questions, clues to help students see that rules and definitions begin with language and are not handed down from some invisible legislature.

The exercises that follow each lesson rely on both traditional and not-so-traditional approaches. As in most grammar books, we give students sentences and ask them to pick out various points of grammar; but as often as possible we also provide opportunities for students to respond more creatively, using what they have learned. For example, students may be asked to follow sentence patterns, write their own sentences, choose effective modifiers, or combine sentences. Teachers can assign all exercises at the time a concept is introduced, assign the identification problems to diagnose weaknesses, or even save some exercises for those occasions when specific problems occur in student writing.

The lessons are arranged in a way that has worked well with our students. Frequently lessons build on each other: the lesson on the compound sentence appears not long after students have learned what constitutes a sentence and right after they have been introduced to the conjunction. Teachers should feel free, however, to skip around or to supplement in areas where students need more follow-up work. The comprehensive exercises may be used to supplement, to diagnose, or to evaluate.

We hope this book begins a discovery for students which will end only when they can use clear, correct, and effective language to express their ideas.

1. NOUNS

In the following sentences, underline any words that name people, animals, places, things, ideas, or feelings:

1. <u>Jane</u> moved to <u>St. Louis</u>.
2. The <u>hiker</u> saw a <u>bear</u> in the <u>forest</u>.
3. <u>Hate</u> is a dangerous <u>emotion</u>.
4. The <u>company</u> sent <u>Ms. Wilson</u> to <u>Italy</u> to sell <u>goldfish</u>.
5. <u>Dan</u> baked a <u>cake</u> for his <u>friends</u>.
6. The <u>girl</u> received the bad <u>news</u> with great <u>courage</u>.

Do you know what the underlined words are called? If you answered *nouns*, you're right.

Definition

A **noun** is a word that names a person, animal, place, thing, idea, or feeling. There are different kinds of nouns.

A **common noun** is a word that names a general class or category of persons, places, or things and is not capitalized. In the above sentences, *hiker*, *bear*, *forest*, *hate*, and *news* are all examples of common nouns.

A **proper noun**, on the other hand, names a specific person, place, or thing and is spelled with a capital letter. *Jane*, *St. Louis*, *Ms. Wilson*, and *Dan* are all examples of proper nouns in the above sentences.

A **collective noun** is a single word that names a group or collection of persons, places, or things. Here are some examples of collective nouns: *jury*, *crowd*, *herd*, *company*, and *mob*.

If two or more words are used to describe a particular person, place, or thing (*high school*, *living room*, *soda fountain*, *ice cream*), they are treated as one noun. Titles such as *Tom Sawyer* or *Treasure Island* are also considered to be one item and treated as a single noun.

SINGULAR/PLURAL

A noun may either be **singular** (one thing) or **plural** (more than one) in form. To form the plural of a noun, you usually add *s* or *es* to the end of the singular form:

rat/rats	peach/peaches
car/cars	potato/potatoes
echo/echoes	exercise/exercises

For some nouns, you will need to change letters when forming the plural:

wolf/wolves	elf/elves
baby/babies	mystery/mysteries
goose/geese	woman/women

The singular and plural forms of a few nouns are the same:

> sheep   fish   deer   salmon

HINT

A. Certain clues will help you identify nouns. For instance, words that come right before the verb (action word) in a sentence are often nouns:

1. The tall <u>girl</u> won the race.
2. <u>Jack</u> read the book three times.
3. My <u>grandma</u> wishes it never rained.

B. Also , the three articles—*a, an,* and *the* —signal that a noun will follow:

1. The man in the red coat is a <u>musician</u>.
2. The hawk killed the <u>mouse</u>.
3. Bill eats an <u>apple</u> every morning.

NOUN EXERCISES

A. *Directions:* Underline the nouns in the following sentences.
EXAMPLE: <u>Tina</u> loves <u>gum</u> and <u>ice cream</u>.

LIFE OF THE HOBO

1. <u>Hoboes</u> traveled from <u>place</u> to <u>place</u> and worked in temporary <u>jobs</u>.
2. <u>Hoboes</u> were sometimes called *migratory* <u>workers</u>.
3. In <u>1900</u> many <u>hoboes</u> traveled around the <u>United States</u> on the <u>railroads</u>.
4. These <u>men</u> did not buy <u>tickets</u> but rode in empty <u>boxcars</u> on freight <u>trains</u>.

5. Hundreds of hoboes were killed or hurt on these dangerous rides.
6. Hoboes often spent the night in camps called "jungles."
7. In the winter many hoboes flocked to cities to seek shelter.
8. Hoboes often composed songs and poems about their journeys.
9. Some migratory workers even published their thoughts and opinions in a magazine called *Hobo News*.
10. The life of a hobo could sometimes be sad and lonely.

B. *Directions:* Some words can be used in more than one way. Underline the words below that could be used as nouns.

EXAMPLE: <u>fear</u>   though   not

to	London	Queen Elizabeth
apple	intelligence	slowly
and	appear	clam
love	orange	red
skunk	into	fish
ugly	song	courage
hope	never	seem
Raymond	mile	river
from	but	frost
idea	month	borrow

C. *Directions:* Insert nouns in the blanks in the following sentences.

EXAMPLE: The ____clams____ are delicious.

1. What kind of _____ does _____ like best?

2. The _____ is going to _____ for a _____.

3. The _____ in the _____ is creating a _____.

4. _____ believes that _____ is the most important quality a person can have.

5. Some _____ don't eat _____ in the _____.

6. A small _____ sat quietly by the edge of the _____.

7. The _____ took us most of the _____ to complete.

8. Please bring me a _____ from the _____.

9. I saw _____ and _____ from the _____.

10. _____ joined the _____ last _____.

D. *Directions:* Write five sentences of your own and then underline the nouns.

EXAMPLE: <u>Sal</u> ate the <u>plum</u>.

1. _____
2. _____
3. _____
4. _____
5. _____

Patrick was jumping the rope

the clock was ticking very slowly

<u>Object</u> recives the action

Bob ate the d<u>o nut</u>

Sue hit (Tom) in the head

Object

2. PRONOUNS

Read the following sentences:

1. The canary is fierce. It ate the cat.
2. My mother is talented. She is an artist.
3. Cars produce exhaust. They cause pollution.

To what or whom do the words *it*, *she*, and *they* refer? If you think about it, you'll soon see that *it* must refer to *canary*. Then you'll probably figure out that *she* refers to *mother* and that *they* refers to *cars*.

> **Definition**
> A **pronoun** is a word that takes the place of a noun.

As you've just seen, the words *it*, *she*, and *they* in the above sentences take the place of the words *canary*, *mother*, and *cars*. The words that pronouns refer to or take the place of are called **antecedents**. An antecedent is something that *goes before* something else.

There are several different kinds of pronouns, but the most commonly used kind is the **personal pronoun**. A personal pronoun can refer to one or more persons or things:

1. Frank is fast. <u>He</u> is a runner.
2. Jan and Liz live next door. <u>They</u> are my friends.
3. The skate needs sharpening. <u>It</u> is too dull.

Personal pronouns also have different forms, depending on whether they are subjects (I, you, he, she, it, we, they) or objects (me, you, him, her, it, us, them). You'll be learning more about subjects and objects in later lessons.

POSSESSIVE PRONOUNS

Some personal pronouns show possession or ownership and act like adjectives. These pronouns are sometimes referred to as **possessive pronouns**. For instance, in the sentence, "Joe is your uncle," the pronoun *your* shows possession and therefore is a possessive pronoun. Other possessive pronouns are: *my, mine, yours, his, her, hers, its, our, ours, their, theirs.*

Now read the following sentences and fill in the blanks with the appropriate pronoun:

1. Alice bought a murder mystery. _____ was scary.

2. The teacher is here, Ramon. _____ had better be quiet.

3. My parents' oldest child is a boy. He is _____ brother.

4. Ms. Casey won the election. _____ celebrated with friends.

5. My guests arrived early. I gave _____ something to eat.

6. The people next door never lock their back door. A burglar got into _____ house and stole _____ camera.

HINT If you have trouble with any of the sentences above, look at the following chart for help.

SINGULAR

	Subjects	Objects	Possessives
1st person	I	me	my, mine
2nd person	you	you	your, yours
3rd person	he, she, it	him, her, it	his, her, hers, its

PLURAL

	Subjects	Objects	Possessives
1st person	we	us	our, ours
2nd person	you	you	your, yours
3rd person	they	them	their, theirs

PRONOUN EXERCISES

A. *Directions:* Circle the pronouns in the following sentences. Underline the nouns.

EXAMPLE: (He) stole my <u>cookie</u> and ate (it.)

1. Aunt Emily bought her a book for Christmas.
2. They packed their bags and left town quickly.
3. Do you think you could find his name in the phone book?
4. Please save us from her ferocious hamsters!
5. I think she likes me better than your brother.
6. She hoped that she would see them on the way to the park.
7. Sue saw him cheating when she raised her head.
8. We did not want to hurt its wings.
9. Those funny-looking slippers you saw are mine.
10. How did he know their friends would not get there on time?

B. *Directions:* In the spaces at the end of each sentence, write the pronouns you would use to replace the italicized nouns.

EXAMPLE: *Ralph* gave the *dog* a bone. _____He_____ _____it_____

1. *Gillian* bought *Trevor* a pet gorilla. _____ _____

2. The *hikers* stopped to watch an *eagle* catch a mouse. _____
_____

3. *Mrs. Rodriguez* confiscated *Billy's* hat during the concert.
_____ _____

4. The *girls* did not like the *novel's* ending. _____ _____

5. The *family's* house disappeared when the *witch* cast a spell.
_____ _____

6. The *lion* watched the *gazelles* with great interest. _____
_____

7. The *rabbit* grabbed the *hunter's* gun and ran away. _____
_____

8. The *audience* applauded when the *movie* ended. _____
_____

9. Joe borrowed the *car* from the *Parkers'* garage. _____
_____

10. *Mr. McGiver* baked the *girl* a carrot cake. _____ _____

C. *Directions:* Circle the pronouns in the list below that show possession.

EXAMPLE: (her)   I   us

our	you	his
he	mine	me
your	their	she
hers	it	its
we	they	my

D. *Directions:* Rewrite the following sentences, replacing the italicized pronouns with nouns.

EXAMPLE: *He* wrote *her* a letter.
　　　　Biff wrote Minnie a letter.

1. *He* wished that *her* father were a nicer person.

_____

2. *She* watched *them* jump out of the water.

_____

3. The reason *they* left *it* behind is not clear.

_____

4. *Their* faces fell when they saw *her* coming.

_____

5. *It* was the last place *he* wanted to be.

_____

Subject pronouns (do action)

I   He   She   they   you   we   it

Object pronouns hit
(receive the action)

hit   Hits   hit   hit   hit hit

Me   him her them you us it

Object

#Possessive pronouns   My   his   her their your our its
(show ownership
act like an
adj)   mine   his   hers theirs yours ours its
myself   himself   herself themselves yourself)
ourselves
itself

#2 Possessive pronouns
stand alone

reflective or intensive pronouns
(a person does the action to)
himself
to stress
who did it

3. VERBS *Patrick*

Read the following sentence and circle the word that tells what Sarah did:

Sarah (hit) the ball through the window.

If you circled *hit*, you're right. Now read the following sentence and circle the word that tells you something about Mr. Belinsky's feeling of sadness:

Mr. Belinsky (seemed) sad.

If you circled *seemed*, you're right again. The word *seemed* tells you something **about** Mr. Belinsky's sadness. He may or may not have actually been sad. What you know for sure is that he **seemed**—or appeared to be—sad.

Definition

The words *hit* and *seemed* in the above sentences are **verbs**. A **verb** is a word that expresses an action (*run, hurl, swim, fly, sing*) or a state of being (*is, appear, seem, be*). The verb is sometimes called the **predicate**. It either tells you what a noun is doing or provides you with information about the state or condition of that noun. Most verbs are **action verbs**. The much smaller group of verbs that express a state of being are called **linking verbs**. You will be learning more about linking verbs later in this series.

Now circle the verbs in the following sentences:

1. Brian (drove) the car (into) a ditch.
2. Sharon (is an excellent) engineer.
3. The bubbles (floated) down (to) the ground.
4. That shaggy dog (looks) happy.

Depending on how they are used, verbs make statements (Sally *walked* to the store.), ask questions (Are you *going* to the concert?), or give commands. (*Give* me that kangaroo!) Read the following sentences and write *statement*, *question*, or *command* in the space provided, depending on what the verb is doing:

1. May I have a drink of water? *question*
2. Throw me that towel. *command*
3. Janice won the marathon. *statement*

HELPING VERBS

Sometimes a verb is preceded by an **auxiliary** or **helping verb**. (Sandy **might** go to the beach.) These helping verbs help the main verb explain in more detail what a noun is doing. For instance, the helping verb *might* in the above sentence tells you that Sandy **may** go to the beach, not that she will definitely go. The verb and its helping verbs together are called **verb phrases**. Circle the verb phrases in the following sentences:

1. I (will fly) to Costa Rica tomorrow.
2. Bob (had read) the book before.
3. Shirley (has been living) in France.
4. Mr. Graham (may have been) mistaken.

As you see, a verb may have one, two, or even three helping verbs. Some of the most common of these helping verbs are: *has, have, had, is, be, been, do, does, did, may, might, will, shall, would,* and *must.*

TENSE

Read the following sentences and write **present**, **past**, or **future** in the spaces provided, depending on when the action took place:

1. Alice will fly the plane next Wednesday. _future_
2. Bill saw the buffalo last summer. _Past_
3. Now the fly buzzes on the windowsill. _Present_
4. Ramon caught the mouse. _Past_
5. Mr. McGovern will travel around China this summer.
future
6. The car speeds around the corner. _Present_

The **tense** of a verb tells you when the action or state of being took place. The three most important tenses are the **present** (It's happening right now: She walks.), the **past** (It already happened: She walked.), and the **future** (It's going to happen—it hasn't happened yet: She will walk.)

The present tense usually ends with *s*. To form the future tense, you use the helping verbs *will* or *shall* with a main verb. To form the past tense, you generally add the letters −*ed*, −*d*, or −*t* to a verb.

Verbs that form the past tense in a different way are **irregular verbs**. To form the past tense of an irregular verb, you must either change a vowel or make other changes in the spelling of the verb. Here are some examples of regular and irregular verbs:

REGULAR		IRREGULAR	
Present	*Past*	*Present*	*Past*
borrow	borrowed	swim	swam
taste	tasted	bring	brought
attack	attacked	throw	threw
arrange	arranged	go	went
chatter	chattered	fly	flew

Now try to list as many irregular verbs as you can on the following lines:

think thought   run ran   blow blew
knew knew   sleep slept   see saw
eat ate   fall fell   make, made
drive drove   drink drank   am was

HINT

A. Two clues will help you identify verbs. First, **helping verbs** such as *will*, *should*, *may*, and *shall* often signal that a main verb will follow:

1. Fred *might eat* at the diner.
2. I *shall see* you next week.

B. Second, if a word makes sense when used after the pronouns *he*, *she*, and *it*, it is probably a verb:

1. He/She/It falls. (verb)
2. He/She/It windows. (*not* a verb)

VERB EXERCISES

A. *Directions:* Underline the verbs in the following sentences twice. Underline the nouns once. Then circle all the pronouns.

EXAMPLE: (She) wrote to the poet.

A GREAT POET

1. John Keats lived most of his life in England.
2. He was born in 1795.
3. Keats had two brothers and a sister.
4. He studied medicine in school but then became a poet.
5. Keats once went on a walking tour of northern England and Scotland.
6. He met William Wordsworth, a famous poet, on several occasions.
7. Keats devoted many hours to his poems and rewrote them many times.
8. Keats died of tuberculosis when he was twenty-five.
9. If he had lived, Keats would have written many more poems.
10. Today, Keats is considered one of the greatest English poets.

B. *Directions:* Insert verbs in the blanks in the following sentences.

EXAMPLE: Gary ___*lifted*___ the bag from the floor.

1. Sam ___gave___ his dog a bowl of water.
2. ___Will___ Courtney ever ___sing___ again?
3. The farmer ___went___ to town and ___sold___ her cattle.
4. I ___might___ ___go___ to the movies on Thursday.
5. Ramon ___skipped___ and ___hopped___ all the way home.
6. The president ___did___ not ___make___ a decision until he ___saw___ all the facts.
7. What ___do___ you ___want___ for your birthday?
8. ___give___ me the article that you ___read___ in the magazine.
9. The tornado ___destroyed___ the town in a few minutes.
10. Lester ___would___ ___have___ ___called___ his father if the concert ___didn't___ ___happen___ .

C. *Directions:* Underline twice the words that could be used as verbs.

    EXAMPLE: <u>scream</u>   now   deep

<u>smack</u>	<u>kiss</u>	elephant
<u>dance</u>	<u>topple</u>	<u>weave</u>
<u>play</u>	yet	<u>stream</u>
gracefully	<u>look</u>	<u>roar</u>
<u>spin</u>	again	<u>sound</u>
rapid	<u>hurt</u>	<u>think</u>
<u>laugh</u>	<u>smell</u>	quickly
boast	<u>feel</u>	<u>sew</u>
<u>ring</u>	<u>wiggle</u>	against
<u>taste</u>	alone	<u>are</u>

D. *Directions:* Using the verb tenses that are indicated, write ten sentences of your own. Then underline the verbs twice.

    EXAMPLE: future   I <u>will go</u> to Paris in May.

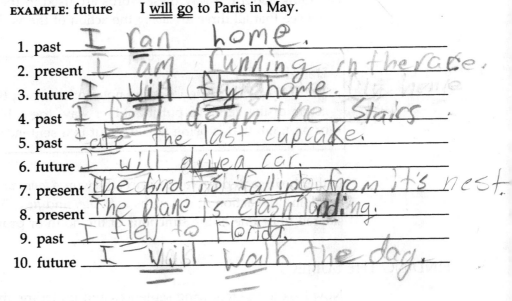

1. past   I ran home.
2. present   I am running in the race.
3. future   I will fly home.
4. past   I fell down the stairs.
5. past   I ate the last cupcake.
6. future   I will drive a car.
7. present   The bird is falling from it's nest.
8. present   The plane is crash landing.
9. past   I flew to Florida.
10. future   I will walk the dog.

4. SUBJECTS

Read the following sentences and then answer the questions in the spaces provided:

1. Jane rode her horse every week.

   Who rode the horse? _____
2. The enormous alligator ate Chicago.

   What ate Chicago? _____
3. The Starskys flew to Rome yesterday.

   Who flew to Rome? _____

What do the three words you wrote in the spaces have in common? If you think about the way these words are used in the above sentences, you'll see that all three are *doing* the action of the verbs.

Definition

The **subject** of a sentence is the noun or pronoun that is doing the action of the verb. To put it another way, the subject is the noun or pronoun that is being talked about in a sentence.

In the above sentences, for instance, the words *Jane, alligator,* and *Starskys* are doing the action of the verbs *rode, ate,* and *flew*. The subject is considered to be one of the **functions** of the noun or pronoun.

FINDING THE SUBJECT

Now look at the following sentences and underline the subjects:

1. The cat in the large dead tree chases birds.
2. The beginning of that book bored me.
3. The top of the building is gold.

As you can see, subjects can often be separated from verbs by several other words. If you're not sure what the subject is, just ask yourself the question, "Who or what is doing the action of the verb?"

The subject of a sentence usually comes before the verb, but it can sometimes come after it. Here are some examples of sentences in which the subjects come after the verbs:

1. There is a <u>gorilla</u> in the kitchen.
2. On the table stood a beautiful <u>bowl</u>.
3. Did <u>Susan</u> buy that tomato?

Notice that the word *there*, which is neither a noun nor pronoun, can never be the subject of a sentence. Also, in sentences that are questions, the subject will usually appear after the helping verb and before the main verb. If you are having trouble finding the subject of a question, changing it into a statement will sometimes help:

<u>Susan</u> bought that tomato.

Now underline the subjects of the following sentences:

1. Buy me a newspaper.
2. Pick up all that trash.

If you can't find the subjects in these sentences, don't worry. In sentences that express commands, the subject "you" is *implied* rather than expressed. In other words, what the person speaking the above sentences is really saying is: "You, buy me a newspaper" and "You, pick up all that trash." *You* is the subject of both sentences, which are commands.

SENTENCES

> **Definition**
> Subjects and verbs are the building blocks of **sentences**. A **sentence** is a group of words that contains a subject and verb and expresses a complete thought. In its most basic form, this complete thought is called an **independent clause** or **simple sentence**.

Sentences that make statements are called **declarative sentences**; sentences that ask questions are called **interrogative sentences**; and sentences that give commands are called **imperative sentences**:

1. Josiah likes scrambled eggs. (declarative)
2. Can the gorilla stay for dinner? (interrogative)
3. Do your grammar homework. (imperative)

SUBJECT EXERCISES

A. *Directions:* Write the subject of each sentence in the space at the end.
   EXAMPLE: The cat ate the mouse. _____*cat*_____

1917: A REMARKABLE YEAR

1. Many important events occurred in 1917. _____

2. The first Russian Revolution ended the rule of the tsars in February. _____

3. President Woodrow Wilson began his second term of office the following month. _____

4. The United States entered World War I that spring.
   _____

5. T. S. Eliot's poem, "The Love Song of J. Alfred Prufrock," stunned the literary world that year. _____

6. Many other brilliant young poets died on the battlefields in France.
   _____

7. John F. Kennedy was born in his family's house in Brookline, Massachusetts. _____

8. Puerto Ricans were granted United States citizenship.
   _____

9. In October, Lenin led a second revolution in Russia.
   _____

10. There are many reasons to spend time reading about that year in history books. _____

B. *Directions:* Insert subjects in the blanks in the following sentences.
   EXAMPLE: _____*Arnie*_____ raced Jan to the corner.

1. _____ flew to Moscow on a peace mission.

2. _____ reached out calmly and yanked me into the boat.

3. _____ followed Sally home at the end of the day.

4. _____ is the title of a famous book.

5. _____ rattled the windows at the height of the storm.

6. _____ made me jump in surprise.

7. _____ knew that I was coming to town on Thursday.

8. Did _____ write a terrifying book about vampires?

9. _____ sang a song until the baby fell asleep.

10. _____ tasted even worse than usual.

C. *Directions:* Use each of the following words as the subject of a sentence.
EXAMPLE: rat   *The rat slithered down the hole.* _____

1. dentist _____

2. calendar _____

3. sunset _____

4. Argentina _____

5. honesty _____

6. photograph _____

7. president _____

8. computer _____

9. Alexis _____

10. alligator _____

D. *Directions:* Write five sentences that begin with *there*. Then write the subject at the end of each sentence.
EXAMPLE: There goes the train.   *train*

1. _____

2. _____

3. _____

4. _____

5. _____

5. CAPITALIZATION

What is wrong with the following sentence?

on monday i bought ms. caruso a book about the american civil war.

It probably didn't take you long to notice that the sentence is missing its capital letters. Here is how it should look:

On Monday I bought Ms. Caruso a book about the American Civil War.

> **Definition**
> In general, **capitalization** is used to signal or set off "beginnings" and proper nouns.

For instance, always capitalize the first word of a sentence, the first word of a direct quotation, and the first word of a line of traditional poetry. Unless you are e. e. cummings,* always capitalize the pronoun *I*, too:

1. The car ran into a tree.
2. John Donne once said, "No man is an island."
3. I love to rise in a summer morn
   When the birds sing on every tree;
4. Why didn't I ever learn to sing?

PROPER NOUNS

In addition to "beginnings," always capitalize proper nouns. As you probably remember from the noun section, proper nouns are nouns that refer to a specific person, place, or thing. Proper nouns include such categories as people's names and titles (if the title goes with the name):

Theodore Roosevelt　　President Truman　　Senator Kennedy

the names of days, months, and holidays:

Wednesday　　February　　Yom Kippur

the names of historical events, periods, and documents:

Great Depression　　Progressive Era　　Magna Carta

*e. e. cummings (1894–1962) was an American poet who did not use capital letters.

the names of cities, states, and countries:

Minneapolis   Montana   Australia

the names of deities, religions, and religious organizations:

Jehovah   Hinduism   National Council of Churches

the names of political parties, governing bodies, and governmental departments:

Republican party   Provisional Government
U.S. Justice Department

the names of races, peoples, and languages:

Hispanic   Chinese   Italian

TITLES AND LETTERS

Titles must always be capitalized. This rule applies to books (*Pride and Prejudice*), poems ("The Road Not Taken"), plays (*Romeo and Juliet*), articles ("Travels through Georgia"), stories ("To Build a Fire"), magazines (*The New Yorker*), newspapers (*Washington Post*), essays ("Shooting an Elephant"), movies (*Star Wars*), songs ("Blue Suede Shoes"), works of art (*Mona Lisa*), and television programs (*Friends*). In titles, capitalize the first and last words and all other words expect prepositions, conjunctions, and articles (*a, an, the*): (*Diary of a Madman and Other Stories*).

Finally, when you are writing a letter, capitalize the first word and all nouns in the salutation or greeting. On the other hand, only capitalize the first word in the closing:

Dear President Lincoln: Yours truly,
Dear Tim and Cindy,   Best wishes,

CAPITALIZATION EXERCISES

A. *Directions:* In the following sentences, circle the letters that should be capitalized.

EXAMPLE: (m)s. (g)omez said that (m)t. (w)ashington is located in (n)ew (h)ampshire.

1. my uncle jack lives on elm street in denver.
2. the empire state building was once the tallest building in new york.
3. the boston red sox play baseball in fenway park.

4. *swallows and amazons* is bill's favorite book.
5. nadine's family usually goes to maine in may or september.
6. the beatles had a hit song called "help."
7. winston churchill was prime minister of england during world war II.
8. dr. chavez grew up in managua, nicaragua.
9. "my papa's waltz" is a poem by theodore roethke.
10. hilary paddled the canoe along the mississippi river from minneapolis to new orleans.

B. *Directions:* Rewrite each word or group of words, properly capitalized, in the space to the right. If the word or group of words is already capitalized properly, just write *C* in the space.
EXAMPLE: los angeles ___*Los Angeles*___

1. mister billingsgate _____
2. *The Name Of The Rose* _____
3. Orthodontist _____
4. mt. mckinley _____
5. *New York Times* _____
6. prime minister Thatcher _____
7. Smallpox _____
8. *The Sword in the Stone* _____
9. Salmon _____
10. lake superior _____
11. Romeo and Juliet _____
12. easter Sunday _____
13. Chicago cubs _____
14. the wind in the willows _____
15. secretary of State _____

C. *Directions:* In the space to the right of each common noun, write a proper noun that is an example of that common noun. Be sure to capitalize the proper noun correctly.
EXAMPLE: pirate ___*Long John Silver*___

1. country _____
2. novel _____
3. river _____

4. singer _____

5. president _____

6. ocean _____

7. month _____

8. poet _____

9. city _____

10. actress _____

6. END PUNCTUATION

Read the following sentences and insert punctuation marks where needed:

1. Trudy ate the whole box of candies
2. Did you enjoy the movie
3. Watch out for that monster

The first sentence is a *statement* and should end in a *period*. The second sentence is a *question* and should end in a *question mark*. The third sentence is an *exclamation* (It expresses a strong or sudden feeling.) and should end in an *exclamation point*.

Definition
Periods, **question marks**, and **exclamation points** are all types of **end punctuation**. They are called end punctuation, not surprisingly, because they appear at the end of a sentence. Just as a capital letter signals the beginning of a sentence, a period, question mark, or exclamation point signals the end of a sentence.

You have already been introduced to imperative sentences (commands) in earlier lessons. As you may have noticed already, commands are punctuated in the same way as statements—with periods:

1. Fetch me the milk.
2. Stop that whining.
3. Look in the basement.

Indirect questions are sentences in which a question is referred to rather than asked directly. Indirect questions also end in periods:

1. Indirect: *Sue asked John if he wanted to go to the dance.*
   Direct: *Sue asked, "Do you want to go to the dance, John?"* ends in a question mark.
2. Indirect: *Tilly asked the mechanic why her car wasn't ready.*
   Direct: *"Why isn't my car ready?" Tilly asked.*

END PUNCTUATION EXERCISES

A. *Directions:* Complete the following sentences by inserting the proper form of end punctuation.
   EXAMPLE: When are we going to the movie?

1. That restaurant is always crowded on weekends
2. What kind of money do they use in Nepal
3. John Wilkes Booth shot Abraham Lincoln at the Ford Theater
4. Watch out for the train
5. Do you think there is any reason to shout
6. An American writer named Ambrose Bierce disappeared in 1914
7. Ralph, catch the baby
8. Reykjavik is the capital of Iceland
9. Would you consider going to the dance with Josie
10. I can't stop the car

B. *Directions:* If a sentence is punctuated correctly, write **C** in the space at the end of the sentence. If the end punctuation is incorrect, circle it and write the correct punctuation in the space.
EXAMPLE: Did Jane drive the car to the movies ___?___

1. Mao Zedong led a revolution in China in 1949! ____
2. What would you like to do with your life. ____
3. Walter spent the summer in Mexico City. ____
4. I can't stand it anymore. ____
5. Did Mr. Pringle believe your story about losing your homework?

____
6. Pip is the main character of the novel *Great Expectations*? ____
7. Get out of my way! ____
8. In 1860, millions of buffalo roamed the American prairies! ____
9. How did Harold lose the goldfish. ____
10. St. Patrick is the patron saint of Ireland? ____

C. *Directions:* Write two statements, two questions, and two exclamations. Punctuate each of these sentences with the proper end punctuation.
EXAMPLE: You're stepping on my hand!

1. _____
2. _____
3. _____
4. _____
5. _____
6. _____

7. COMMAS

What could you do to the following sentence to make it clearer?

Betty bring me a cup plate and bowl.

Now compare what you did with the following version of the sentence:

Betty, bring me a cup, plate, and bowl.

Inserting three commas into the above sentence makes the meaning of the sentence much clearer. You can tell that somebody is speaking to Betty and asking her to bring three separate items rather than a "cup plate" and a "bowl."

Definition
The **comma** is the most frequently used form of punctuation, and it helps you to make sense out of a sentence. In other words, commas—as you've already seen above—make it easier to read and understand sentences. Commas are used either alone or in pairs. When used alone, they set off or *separate* items. (I'll see you later, Ralph.) When used in pairs, they *enclose* items. (On Tuesday, October 4, I won a million dollars.)

SERIES

Use commas to separate a series of three or more items:

1. Jack put mustard, ketchup, and relish on his hot dog.
2. Mrs. Beazley walked, ran, and skipped to the store.
3. Brook saw lions, tigers, bears, and wizards in the woods.

Although leaving out the comma before the word *and* is also considered to be correct, this practice can sometimes lead to confusion:

June read books about soldiers, sailors, cops and robbers.

It is not clear from this sentence whether June read books about three or four subjects. Since you can *always* avoid this kind of confusion when you use the comma before the word *and* in a series, we recommend that you use it.

BETWEEN ADJECTIVES

Commas that are used to separate adjectives take the place of the word *and*. If you can insert the word *and* between two adjectives, use a comma. If you can't insert the word *and*, do not use a comma:

1. the small, graceful dancer (The *small and graceful dancer* makes sense.)
2. the bright young man (The *bright and young man* does *not* make sense.)
3. the heavy, clumsy dog (The *heavy and clumsy dog* makes sense.)
4. the enthusiastic senior class (The *enthusiastic and senior class* does *not* make sense.)

HINT When you can insert *and* between two adjectives and it makes sense, there is usually a natural pause between the two words. It is sometimes useful to read the phrase out loud to yourself to see if you can hear this pause. If you hear a pause, insert a comma.

INTRODUCTORY WORDS

Use commas after words like *oh, well, yes,* and *no* when they come at the beginning of a sentence:

1. Oh, why can't you be quiet?
2. Yes, I see your point.
3. Well, of course I know Sally's mother.

DIRECT ADDRESS

Use commas to set off or enclose words that are used to address or speak to a person:

1. Mom, please give me a dollar.
2. Come here, Roxanne, and look at this frog.
3. I can't find your horse, Slim.

MISUNDERSTANDING

Sometimes it is necessary to use commas to prevent misunderstanding or misreading:

To Emily William was a fool.

This sentence isn't about a girl named Emily William, as you might first think. If you add a comma after *Emily*, you'll see the sentence reveals

Emily's opinion of William. Sentences 1 and 2 would also be confusing without commas:

1. After seeing his uncle, Bill bought a paper.
2. Above, the jet roared through the sky.

When you try reading these sentences without commas, you'll see that it is possible to misread them.

DATES, ADDRESSES, AND GEOGRAPHICAL NAMES

Use commas to separate items in dates, addresses, and geographical names:

1. Tuesday, June 29, 1901
2. 6 Duck Street, Grinnell, Iowa
3. Paris, France

LETTERS

Use commas after the salutation of a friendly or informal letter (as opposed to a business letter) and after the closing of any letter:

> Dear Aunt May,   Yours truly,
> Dear Dad,   Sincerely,

There are a number of other situations in which it is necessary to use commas. You will learn about these situations as you study new concepts later in these books.

COMMA EXERCISES

A. *Directions:* Insert commas where they are needed in the following sentences.
EXAMPLE: By the way, Shirley, how's your parakeet?

1. Gabriela wanted bacon lettuce and tomato on her sandwiches.
2. No I do not want to go to the lecture on dinosaurs.
3. Is that you Makiba?
4. When she saw her aunt Martha began to laugh.
5. The spy gave Herman a cold murderous look.
6. Does Mr. Kaplinsky live in Kansas City Kansas or Kansas City Missouri?
7. John Kennedy was assassinated on November 22 1963.
8. Above the eagle flew gracefully through the air.
9. The bright young man sat down ordered his breakfast and ate it.

10. Oh why won't you ever listen to me Thelma?
11. To Betty Henry looked like a clown.
12. Robert loved to read books by Gogol Turgenev Tolstoy and Chekhov.
13. His smooth graceful walk revealed that he was a dancer.
14. Ever since Sam has been scared of angry muskrats.
15. Yes Rosie I intend to visit Rome Italy.

B. *Directions:* Insert commas where they are needed in the following sentences. If a sentence is correct, write the letter **C** in the space at the end.
   EXAMPLE: Please bring me a drink, Tim. _C_

   1. Well I don't see why they moved to Houston, Texas. _____

   2. Nigel's favorite colors were black gray, and white. _____

   3. Roy, could you help me mow the lawn on Friday June 10? _____

   4. The cool, green water lapped around Matilda's feet. _____

   5. Yes, I think I will go swimming on Mondays Wednesdays and Saturdays. _____

   6. Now will you roll the dice and move, Billy? _____

   7. Leroy lived at 6 Oakhurst Drive Springfield, Ohio. _____

   8. Running, reading, and fishing were Anne's favorite activities.
   _____

   9. No, Elvida you can't put marshmallows in the soup. _____

   10. According to his uncle Harry was a mean, unfriendly boy. _____

C. *Directions:* In the following sentences, circle the commas that are not necessary and insert commas where they are needed.
   EXAMPLE: Jane‸lived in an old‚shabby house.

   1. Penelope collects butterflies coins, bumper stickers, and, stamps.
   2. The athletic, senior girls live in Spokane Washington.
   3. Next to her, cousin Jake June saw an enormous turtle.
   4. Well Phillip, I guess, reading writing and math are not your strong points.
   5. Woody Guthrie, grew up in Okemah Oklahoma.
   6. Donald saw a group of large, hungry, crocodiles slip into the river.
   7. He arrived, in Flatfoot North Dakota on May 12, 1972.
   8. No I don't believe a word, you are saying Alice.
   9. Gum drops chocolate and boiled, sweets are all examples of candy.
   10. When, did you become a lawyer Arturo?

D. *Directions:* Make up sentences that illustrate each of the following situations.

EXAMPLE: commas in dates ___I was born on August 4, 1923.___

1. commas in series _____

_____

2. commas between adjectives _____

_____

3. commas to prevent misunderstandings _____

_____

4. commas after opening words _____

_____

5. commas in direct address _____

_____

6. commas in addresses _____

_____

8. SENTENCE FRAGMENTS

Which of the following groups of words are sentences?

1. In an old, dark cottage at the end of an autumn day.
2. Running through the town on Monday.
3. When Ann heard the angry dog.

Although the above groups of words look like sentences, you may have figured out that none of them actually is a sentence. Two of them are missing a subject and a verb, and all three of them leave you up in the air as to what is going to happen. These words are fragments—incomplete pieces of sentences.

> **Definition**
> As you learned earlier, a sentence is a group of words that contains a subject and verb and expresses a complete thought. A sentence also must begin with a capital letter and end in some type of end punctuation. A **sentence fragment**, on the other hand, is a group of words that does *not* express a complete thought. Fragments, such as the examples above, do not finish the ideas or thoughts they begin. In other words, they leave you hanging.

TYPES OF FRAGMENTS

Some sentence fragments are easy to spot because they don't contain subjects and verbs:

1. Living in the country.
2. The woman on the camel.
3. All around the tower of the church.

Other sentence fragments contain subjects and verbs but still do not express a complete thought:

1. After she finished the book.
2. Although Amy disagreed with the president.
3. Before I play the piano again.

TURNING FRAGMENTS INTO SENTENCES

Now look back at the three sentence fragments at the beginning of this lesson. Add whatever words are necessary to turn these fragments into complete sentences. Then write your sentences in the following spaces:

1. _____
2. _____
3. _____

SENTENCE FRAGMENT EXERCISES

A. *Directions:* In the space following each group of words, write *F* if it is a fragment and *S* if it is a sentence.
EXAMPLE: Sam didn't know what. _*F*_

1. At the beginning of the game on Tuesday. _____
2. When Mitzi arrived home from the movie. _____
3. I bought a cat yesterday. _____
4. With a gleam in her eye and a toss of her head. _____
5. Ed cried. _____
6. Why must you always on Thursday? _____
7. If I had a model train set. _____
8. Before Bea had a chance to call her name. _____
9. I suppose I haven't expressed myself clearly. _____
10. Skimming above the surface of the water a beautiful fish. _____

B. *Directions:* Rewrite the following fragments so that they are sentences. Be sure to use every word of the fragment in your sentence.
EXAMPLE: If you eat that toadstool.
 If you eat that toadstool, you might die.

1. Whenever I see a grizzly bear.

 _____

2. My favorite rock performer in the world.

 _____

3. In a dusty corner at the back of the attic.

 _____

4. Running through the woods on a cold winter morning.

 _____

5. Although Janice had never been to Norway before.

   _____

6. Because I was late for my first class.

   _____

7. Hoping that the bus hadn't left without her.

   _____

8. While we were setting up your tent in the woods.

   _____

9. In the event of a flood or tornado.

   _____

10. Before you read that book about South Africa.

    _____

C. *Directions:* Read the following sentence fragments. In the space at the end of each fragment, write *yes* if the fragment contains a subject and verb and *no* if the fragment does not contain a subject and verb.
   EXAMPLE: When I saw the fox. _yes_

   1. At the end of a long day in the mountains. _____
   2. Even if you do catch the frog. _____
   3. Since you insist on choosing the turkey. _____
   4. Above the beautiful, swift river. _____
   5. On top of the bowl of cornflakes. _____
   6. Swimming in the slimy river. _____
   7. Through the dark tunnel out into the sunlight. _____
   8. Because you do not like the mail carrier. _____
   9. When Carl feeds the peacock. _____
   10. In the quietest part of the recital. _____

9. RUN-ON SENTENCES

How many sentences does the following group of words contain?

Marc went to town he bought a soda, then he walked home.

If you answered *one*, look again. The above group of words actually contains three complete thoughts and three sets of subjects and verbs. If properly capitalized and punctuated, these words should look like this:

Marc went to town. He bought a soda. Then he walked home.

Definition

A **run-on sentence** consists of two or more sentences that are linked together without the correct punctuation. It is not a proper sentence because it doesn't stop when it should.

To correct run-ons, you must insert end punctuation and capital letters where they are needed. Look at the following run-on sentences and then look at the corrected versions of these sentences:

1a. The bird ate the worm afterwards, it flew away. (run-on)
 b. The bird ate the worm. Afterwards, it flew away. (two sentences)

2a. Claudette caught two trout her mother helped her clean them they ate the fish for dinner. (run-on)
 b. Claudette caught two trout. Her mother helped her clean them. They ate the fish for dinner. (three sentences)

HINT In order to avoid run-on sentences, it is important to look carefully at each sentence you write. If a sentence contains more than one idea, or if it contains several subjects and verbs, it might be a run-on. Be sure to use the proper end punctuation at the conclusion of each sentence and a capital letter at the beginning of each new one.

RUN-ON SENTENCE EXERCISES

A. *Directions:* In the space following each group of words, write *R* if it is a run-on sentence and *S* if it is a sentence.

EXAMPLE: Eric ran to town he missed the bus. _R_

1. Socrates was a famous Greek philosopher. _____
2. Dan met Sue on the bus then they went to the beach. _____
3. The bear chased Stephanie, she climbed a tree just in time. _____
4. We have seen the movie before, we'd like to go again. _____
5. I don't believe in eating pretzels with a fork. _____
6. Mr. Rochester hired Jane Eyre to be a governess she fell in love with him. _____
7. Dark had fallen, it was a stormy night. _____
8. When I go to a play, I like to get there early. _____
9. I do not believe in ghosts, they don't really exist. _____
10. Go dig some clams at the beach bring them back here for dinner. _____

B. *Directions:* Turn the following run-ons into sentences by putting capital letters where sentences should begin and end punctuation where they should end.

EXAMPLE: Helen bought a house. She loved it.

1. My house wasn't the same anymore it even smelled different.
2. We went to the fair every day you could go on three rides for a dollar.
3. Climbing the mountain was hard I would not do it again.
4. Sailing is her favorite sport each weekend she goes to the lake.
5. The magazine finally arrived now I can read my article.
6. The hurricane destroyed the house everyone inside it was saved.
7. You'd have to see it yourself I can't describe it in words.
8. The writer finished his book he began another one right away.
9. Most people buy pumpkins in the fall they carve them for Halloween.
10. The end of the spy story was exciting it kept me on the edge of my seat.

C. *Directions:* In the space after each group of words, write *R* if it is a run-on, *F* if it is a fragment, and *S* if it is a sentence.

EXAMPLE: In the dark woods. *F*

1. Riding out the storm on a cold, wild night. _____
2. After the party, Julie drove home with Miriam. _____
3. Daryl spent two weeks in the Soviet Union she thought it was a fascinating place. _____
4. Franklin Roosevelt won reelection in 1940, a year before the United States entered World War II. _____
5. I think I'll visit Sally maybe she'll want to take a walk. _____
6. Even though I had never seen such a beautiful sunset on a winter day. _____
7. Mamie fell from the tree she broke her arm. _____
8. Martin Luther King led the fight against racial discrimination in the 1950s and 1960s. _____
9. No, I think I'll stay inside, it's too hot to run. _____
10. On the far side of the river, chewing on a tree, the beaver. _____

10. CONTRACTIONS

Combine each of the underlined pairs of words into one word. Then write that word in the space provided:

1. We <u>are not</u> going to the movies after all. _____

2. I <u>have not</u> seen him in a long time. _____

3. <u>I am</u> determined to get my degree. _____

> **Definition**
> The words that you formed above—*aren't*, *haven't*, and *I'm*—are called **contractions**. A **contraction** is a word that is formed by shrinking two words into one. To make a contraction, you must remove one or more letters and add an apostrophe to the place where the letters have been removed. The apostrophe tells you exactly where the missing letters once stood.

Writers generally use contractions in informal or creative writing. It is a good idea to avoid using them in formal essays or compositions. Here are some more examples of contractions:

1. they are   they're
2. she is   she's
3. could not   couldn't
4. we have   we've
5. should not   shouldn't
6. will not   won't*

When you are forming a contraction, be sure to put the apostrophe in the place where the letters have been removed. Also, be sure not to confuse the contractions *it's* (it is) and *you're* (you are) with the possessive pronouns *its* (*its* head) and *your* (*your* car).

---

*As you probably noticed, *won't* is an unusual contraction. To form it, you must change some letters as well as drop some.

If a word is a contraction, you should be able to change it into two words and still have a good sentence:

1. It's a girl.   It is a girl. (makes sense)
2. I saw its tail.   I saw it is tail. (does *not* make sense)
3. You're a great player.   You are a great player. (makes sense)
4. I like your shirt.   I like you are shirt. (does *not* make sense)

CONTRACTION EXERCISES

A. *Directions:* Turn the italicized words in each sentence into a contraction and write it in the space provided at the end.
EXAMPLE: I *do not* like sheep. ___*don't*___

1. I *would not* kiss you if you were the last frog on Mars. _____

2. *They are* not going to New Zealand this year. _____

3. You know *that is* not what I meant. _____

4. Maria *will not* finish the book on time. _____

5. *I would* love to be a painter some day. _____

6. *They have* lived in this town for years. _____

7. Does that mean *you would* see it? _____

8. Bernice *cannot* go on the fact-finding mission to South America. ___

9. The astronauts *are not* flying to the moon in May. _____

10. *They will* have to see the ballet another time. _____

B. *Directions:* Rewrite the following contractions as two words.
EXAMPLE: isn't ___*is*___ ___*not*___

1. wasn't _____ _____

2. I'd _____ _____

3. you've _____ _____

4. shouldn't _____ _____

5. I've _____ _____

6. let's _____ _____

7. didn't _____ _____

8. you'd _____ _____

9. I'm _____ _____

10. hasn't _____ _____

C. *Directions:* Circle the contractions if the apostrophe is not placed correctly. On the blank next to the word, write the letters that are left out. Put the apostrophe in the right place.

EXAMPLE: (w'ere) _a_ _we're_

1. they'll   _____
2. are'nt   _____
3. she's   _____
4. they're   _____
5. wo'nt   _____
6. youv'e   _____
7. he'll   _____
8. shouldn't   _____
9. we'll   _____
10. was'nt   _____
11. you'll   _____
12. ther'es   _____

11. POSSESSIVES

Can you think of a shorter way to write the following phrases? Use the spaces provided to the right of each phrase:

1. the cry of the loon _____

2. the basketball that belongs to the girls _____

3. the novels of Jane Austen _____

If you rewrote the above phrases in the possessive form, here is how they would look:

1. the loon's cry
2. the girls' basketball
3. Jane Austen's novels

> **Definition**
> The **possessive** form of a noun shows possession, ownership, or connection. In the above phrases, for instance, the cry is a noise the loon makes, the basketball belongs to the girls, and the novels were written by Jane Austen.

If you can make an *of* phrase with a noun, you can also use that noun in its possessive form:

1. the president's mistake   (the mistake of the president)
2. the women's club   (the club of the women)
3. the conductor's baton   (the baton of the conductor)

FORMING THE POSSESSIVE

To form the possessive of singular nouns, add *'s* to these nouns:

> dog/dog's   Simon/Simon's   table/table's

For singular nouns that end in *s*, it is also correct to form the possessive by adding the apostrophe only:

> Charles's or Charles'   Brandeis's or Brandeis'
> Jesus's or Jesus'   Dickens's or Dickens'

However, you will *always* be right if you add *'s* to the singular form of a noun.

To form the possessive of plural nouns that end in *s*, just add an apostrophe to these nouns:

teachers'   cities'   writers'

To form the possessive of plural nouns that do *not* end in *s*, add an '*s* to these nouns:

men's   sheep's   children's

HINT Before deciding whether to add an apostrophe or an '*s* to a plural noun, first make sure that you have formed the plural of that noun correctly. As you learned in the lesson on nouns, you will need to change some letters when forming the plurals of certain nouns. When forming the possessive plural of a noun, therefore, first change the noun into its plural form and then make the noun possessive:

Singular	Plural	Possessive Plural
boat	boats	boats'
box	boxes	boxes'
thief	thieves	thieves'
baby	babies	babies'
ox	oxen	oxen's
man	men	men's
deer	deer	deer's

POSSESSIVE EXERCISES

A. *Directions:* Change the italicized words into the possessive form of the noun and then rewrite the phrase in the space provided.

EXAMPLE: the ears *of the dog* ___the dog's ears___

1. roar *of the ocean* _____

2. poems *of John Keats* _____

3. call *of the swan* _____

4. speeches *of the politician* _____

5. music *of Bach* _____

6. whisper *of the wind* _____

7. beauty *of the forest* _____

8. life *of Charles* _____

9. cold *of winter* _____

10. hair *of the woman* _____

B. *Directions:* Fill in the blank in each sentence with the plural possessive form of the noun that appears below the line.

EXAMPLE: He had five _____*days'*_____ rest at home.
<u>day</u>

1. My grandmother belonged to a _____ sewing circle.
   <u>lady</u>

2. The chorus conductor was pleased with the _____ voices.
   <u>man</u>

3. The _____ honks woke Matilda from a sound sleep.
   <u>goose</u>

4. The _____ toys lay scattered around the room.
   <u>child</u>

5. All three _____ airports need to be repaired.
   <u>city</u>

6. The _____ wool is turned into beautiful, warm sweaters.
   <u>sheep</u>

7. The _____ house is really a mansion.
   <u>Jones</u>

8. He looked through the glass window at the _____ faces.
   <u>baby</u>

9. _____ robes are almost always black.
   <u>Judge</u>

10. The _____ howls sent a tingle up Jennifer's spine.
    <u>wolf</u>

C. *Directions:* Insert apostrophes in the correct places in the following sentences.

EXAMPLE: I love Jimmy's new bicycle.

1. The two mens shirts were soaked through after the rain.
2. Jane loved all of E.B. Whites books.
3. The farmers market has the best fruit and vegetables in town.
4. I wish I didn't have to go to my uncles house.
5. Which of the Beatles CDs do you own?
6. All three of the doctors bills were high.
7. The shelves contents were soon emptied by the thieves.
8. My cars engine fell out at the start of my journey.
9. We passed through the hurricanes eye at 4:00.
10. The musicians instruments disappeared after their concert.

D. *Directions:* Change the italicized words into the possessive form of the noun and then rewrite the phrase in the space provided.
EXAMPLE: core *of the apple* ____*the apple's core*____

1. spots *of the ponies* _____
2. death *of the soldier* _____
3. intelligence *of the women* _____
4. den *of the foxes* _____
5. hands *of the clock* _____
6. speed *of the cheetah* _____
7. depth *of the ocean* _____
8. mark *of Cain* _____
9. grace *of the eagles* _____
10. poems *of Robert Burns* _____
11. children *of the McCrumpets* _____
12. bells *of the cathedrals* _____
13. anger *of the mob* _____
14. laughter *of the girls* _____
15. tears *of the crocodile* _____

12. QUOTATION MARKS

How would you punctuate the following sentences to show that Jake and Shirley are speaking?

1. Jake said I wish I had a purple canary.
2. When are you going to Alaska? Shirley asked.

If you added quotation marks to these sentences, then you have the right idea. Here is how they should look:

1. Jake said, "I wish I had a purple canary."
2. "When are you going to Alaska?" Shirley asked.

Definition
Quotation marks are used to indicate the exact words a person is saying—a quote. The words they enclose, or set off, are a **direct quotation**.

Quotation marks come in pairs; it is important that you remember to place one at the beginning and one at the end of a quotation. If a direct quotation is interrupted, and the sentence includes words that are *not* the exact words a person is saying, you will need to use two sets of quotation marks:

1. "I don't know," she said, "who you think you are."
2. "Please be quiet," Tip pleaded, "so that I can hear myself think."

INDIRECT QUOTATIONS

Sometimes a sentence will report what a person said without using that person's exact words. This type of sentence is called an **indirect quotation**. Quotation marks are *not* used to enclose indirect quotations:

1a. Juanita asked Tony to go to the prom with her.   (*indirect*)
 b. Juanita asked, "Will you go to the prom with me, Tony?"   (*direct*)

2a. Herman announced that he didn't feel well.   (*indirect*)
 b. "I don't feel well," Herman announced.   (*direct*)

PLACEMENT OF PUNCTUATION

Use a comma to set off a direct quotation from the rest of the sentence:

1. Gordon said, "I wasn't here yesterday."
2. "I love circuses," Zachary explained.

Always put commas and periods inside the final quotation mark. Place question marks and exclamation points inside the final quotation mark too, *unless* they are *not* part of the actual quotation:

1. "I'm over here," Patricia said.
2. Bill said, "I like to read history books."
3. Gretta asked, "When can I use the car?"
4. "Don't touch that shark!" Bubba screamed.
5. Why did Joanna say, "I believe in equal rights for everyone"? (The question mark is *not* part of the direct quotation, so it goes *outside* the final quotation mark.)

TITLES

In addition to direct quotations, quotation marks are also used to enclose the titles of short stories, short poems, paintings, songs, articles, speeches, chapters, and essays:

"The Lottery" (story)	"Olympia" (painting)
"The Gettysburg Address" (speech)	"A Modest Proposal" (essay)

Certain kinds of titles do *not* get enclosed with quotation marks, however. The titles of books, newspapers, magazines, movies, and television shows are underlined instead:

<u>Chicago Tribune</u> (newspaper)	<u>Newsweek</u> (magazine)
<u>Little Women</u> (book)	<u>Titanic</u> (movie)

QUOTATION MARKS EXERCISES

A. *Directions:* Insert quotation marks where they are needed in the following sentences. Insert all other punctuation as needed, too. If a sentence is correct already, write a **C** after it.
EXAMPLE: "That's my hat," said Ralph. ____

1. What did you bring me from Mexico Alice asked. ____

2. Ernie heard someone say in the silence There goes the ball game.

____

3. Jose said, See you later, and then walked home. _____

4. June said that she had a stomach ache after eating two pizzas. _____

5. Bring me the hammer from the basement, please his mother said. _____

6. I was surprised when the dog said Fetch me a bone. _____

7. The man said Trust me and winked at Max. _____

8. The girl asked me what we were eating for dinner. _____

9. You won't be sorry if you vote for me the politician promised. _____

10. She smiled and answered Of course I like country music. _____

B. *Directions:* Rewrite the following indirect quotations as direct quotations and insert quotation marks where they are needed.
EXAMPLE: Jim said he liked Al's hat.
"I like your hat," Jim said to Al.

1. Leroy said that a huge blizzard is on the way.

_____

2. Mr. Wiggins told me that I'd better get out of the road.

_____

3. That strange boy asked me what time it is.

_____

4. Jane said she is going to India for a month.

_____

5. I said that I had never seen a purple cat before.

_____

6. The manager asked Frank when he intended to start working.

_____

C. *Directions:* The following sentences contain a variety of titles. Following the rules for titles, either enclose these in quotation marks or underline them.

EXAMPLE: Sue played a song called "Freight Train."

1. The Washington Post is one of the best newspapers in the world.
2. One of Sarah's favorite poems is Nothing Gold Can Stay, by Robert Frost.
3. Jack London wrote a story called To Build a Fire.
4. War and Peace is a very long novel.
5. You're the Top is a Cole Porter song.
6. Humphrey Bogart starred in a movie called Casablanca.
7. Stuart read an article entitled How to Double Your Savings in a Day.
8. Sunflowers is one of Van Gogh's most famous paintings.
9. The name of the chapter is The River Bank.
10. I read about her in Harpers magazine.

D. *Directions:* Write a short conversation between two people and insert quotation marks where they are needed.

_____

_____

_____

_____

_____

_____

_____

_____

13. ADJECTIVES

Read the following sentences. Underline the nouns in each sentence once. Then answer the questions in the spaces provided.

A. Four boys stuffed slimy worms into the big buckets.
1. *How many* boys? _4_
2. *What kind* of worms? ~~big~~ slimy
3. *Which* buckets? big buckets

B. For heat, tight-fisted Mr. Scrooge daily used two lumps of bituminous coal.
1. *Which* Mr. Scrooge? tight fisted
2. *How many* lumps of coal? two lumps
3. *What kind* of coal? bituminous

The words you have written in the spaces above modify (describe) other words in three ways. They answer the questions which one? what kind? and how many? *Big* tells which bucket, and *tight-fisted* tells which Mr. Scrooge. *Slimy* tells what kind of worms and *bituminous* tells what kind of coal. *Four* and *two* tell how many boys and how many pieces of coal. Sometimes it is difficult to make a distinction between which one and what kind. *Slimy* could just as easily tell which worms as well as what kind of worms. Both answers would be correct.

Definition
An **adjective** describes or limits a noun or pronoun by telling *which one*, *what kind*, or *how many*.

Adjectives help you to see objects more clearly. For example, *slimy* lets you imagine the feel of the worms. If you were to say *wriggly* or *whip-like*, you could even begin to see the worms move. In the same way, *tight-fisted* creates the image of a Mr. Scrooge who is miserly and un-generous. The more vivid and precise the adjectives you use, the clearer the picture you create.

Now read the italicized sentence below. Underline the nouns once. Then answer the questions in the spaces provided.

In colonial times young girls in needlework schools embroidered many samplers to learn the alphabet and Biblical passages.

1. What words answer *what kind*? _____

2. What words do the answers to 1 describe? _____

3. What word answers *how many*? _____

4. What word does the answer to 3 describe? _____

5. What words answer *which one*? _____

6. What words do the answer to 5 describe? _____

What do the words *samplers, schools, passages, times,* and *girls* have in common? Yes, each has an adjective to describe it. Also, each is the same part of speech: a noun. Remember, adjectives always modify nouns or pronouns.

HINT

A. The adjective is usually located in front of the noun that it modifies.

Maria put on a *dazzling* hat.

B. Nouns sometimes function as adjectives:

Helen put on her *baseball* cap.

In the above sentence, *baseball*, which names something, also describes what kind of cap Helen put on. *Baseball* is a noun functioning as an adjective in this sentence.

C. The three articles (*a, an,* and *the*) always function as adjectives:

I'll use *the* spoon.

The tells which spoon the writer will use.

D. Possessive nouns (such as *Henry's, America's,* and *dog's*) and possessive pronouns (*my, mine, your, yours, his, her, hers, its, our, ours, their,* and *theirs*) always function as adjectives:

Take *Henry's* answers and compare them with *your* answers.

The adjectives *Henry's* and *your* both tell which answers will be compared.

Practice finding the adjectives in the following sentences. Underline and write *adj.* above each adjective.

1. The imaginative Anne Shirley helped shy Matthew and peevish Marilla discover companionship.
2. Tricky Rumpelstiltskin thought he had trapped the hapless spinning girl into giving him her first-born child.
3. Some people think the advertising on children's television programs traps viewers into wanting too many toys.

You should have found four adjectives in the first sentence, five in the second sentence, and four in the last.

ADJECTIVE EXERCISES

A. *Directions:* After each noun, list in the spaces provided three adjectives that precisely and vividly describe it.
   EXAMPLE: oatmeal ___*mushy, beige, lumpy*___

1. feather ___fluffy___
2. diamond ___shiny___
3. fish ___aquatic___
4. sunlight ___bright___
5. school ___acitemic___
6. fire ___hot flickering overheating___
7. snow ___cold___
8. spiders ___hairy___
9. summer ___sunny___
10. friend ___funny___

B. *Directions:* Change the words listed below into adjectives. Write the answers in the spaces provided.
   EXAMPLE: become ___*becoming*___

1. begin _____
2. change _____
3. mercy _____
4. shine _____
5. come _____
6. courtesy _____

7. curiosity _____

8. who _____

9. twelve _____

10. vigor _____

11. they _____

12. ridicule _____

13. religion _____

14. desire _____

15. disaster _____

16. eight _____

17. differ _____

18. imagination _____

19. it _____

20. mischief _____

C. *Directions:* Read each sentence. List all the adjectives (except the articles *a*, *an*, and *the*) in the space provided.

EXAMPLE: The humorous Mr. O'Dell told many jokes.
   humorous   *many*

STRANGE BUT TRUE BASEBALL FACTS

1. The first baseball game was played in Hoboken, New Jersey, on June 19, 1846.

   _____

2. Baseball's basic rules were not created by Abner Doubleday, but by Alexander J. Cartwright.

   _____

3. Cartwright laid out the present dimensions of the playing field.

   _____

4. The first professional team was the Cincinnati Red Stockings.

   _____

5. The Red Stockings toured in 1869, and they had an undefeated season.

   _____

6. In the late 1800s there were different rules.

   _____

7. It took nine balls for a walk instead of today's four balls.

_____

8. A batter could request a high pitch or a low pitch.

_____

9. Pitchers made underhand throws and not overhand ones.

_____

10. The pitching distance from homeplate to the pitcher's mound was forty-five feet and not the sixty feet and six inches of today.

_____

11. The game of baseball has created unbelievable stories.

_____

12. Baseball has no time clock.

_____

13. In 1952, in a famous game between the Brooklyn Dodgers and the Cincinnati Reds, a half-inning lasted one hour.

_____

14. In that one hour the Dodgers scored fifteen runs in twenty-one times at bat.

_____

15. In another instance Cleveland Indians' pitcher, Eddie Lopat won eleven straight victories against the Yankees.

_____

16. In his next game this streak was broken.

_____

17. A Yankees fan dropped a black cat at Lopat's feet and jinxed him.

_____

18. He gave up five runs in the first inning, and the Yankees eventually won.

_____

19. About a hundred years ago, pitcher Fred Goldsmith proved that a curve ball really curves.

_____

20. He placed three poles in a straight line.

_____

21. His pitch skirted the right of the first pole, the left of the second pole, and the right of the third pole.

_____

Patrick

D. *Directions:* Write ten sentences using any adjectives from the right column below to describe a noun from the left column. You may re-use adjectives.

EXAMPLE: voice   scratchy
The scratchy voice travelled through the telephone wire and hit her ear like a rusty knife.

Noun	Adjective
noise	American
teacher	scary
music	wheezy
bus	sixty-five
motorcycle	talking
sight	raspy
goose	eye-dazzling
rainbow	colorful
sandwich	noisy
garden	elderly

1. The American teacher was very scary
2. _____
3. _____
4. _____
5. _____
6. _____
7. _____
8. _____
9. _____
10. _____

14. ADVERBS

Underline the verb twice in each sentence below. Then, in the spaces following each sentence, write the two words from the sentence that tell you something *more* about the verb.

1. James quickly ran away. _____ _____

2. Yesterday Sara played terribly. _____ _____

If you have trouble finding the right words, look for those words that are neither nouns nor verbs. In the first sentence the words *quickly* and *away* give you two pieces of information about the verb: *quickly* tells **how** James ran and *away* tells **where** James ran. In the second sentence *yesterday* tells **when** Sara played and *terribly* tells **how** she played.

Now look at two more sentences. Which word gives you more information about the word *fast* in the first sentence? Which word tells you something more about the word *delicious* in the second sentence?

1. Kianga wanted to get to her grandmother's house very fast. _____

2. Her grandmother gave her some extremely delicious strawberry short-cake. _____

In the above sentences the word *very* modifies (describes) *fast* and the word *extremely* modifies *delicious*. Both words tell **to what extent** or **to what degree** an action is done or a quality is present. We know that Kianga runs, not simply *fast*, but *very fast* (or fast to an extreme extent). We also know that the shortcake was not just *delicious*, but *extremely delicious* (or delicious to an extreme degree).

Definition

The words *quickly, away, yesterday, terribly, very,* and *extremely* in the above sentences are all examples of **adverbs**. An **adverb** is a word that describes or limits a verb, adjective, or other adverb and answers the questions **how, when, where,** or **to what extent.** Adverbs help you describe an action more precisely, more vividly, and more completely.

---

1. Kianga walked to her grandmother's house and knocked on the door.
2. **Today** Kianga walked **briskly** to her grandmother's house and knocked **excitedly** on the door.

You know much more after reading the second sentence than you do after reading the first. You know **when** Kianga walked to her grandmother's; you know **how** she walked there; and you know **how** she knocked on the door. The adverbs *today*, *briskly*, and *excitedly* give you these extra pieces of information.

> ## HINT
>
> A. An adverb usually appears next to the verb, adjective, or adverb that it describes.
>
> Kianga walked *extremely hurriedly*, her *brilliantly* colorful dress billowing behind her.
>
> B. Although a word ending in *-ly* is usually an adverb, it can also be an adjective. Some adjectives ending in *-ly* are: ugly, womanly, lovely, stately, and lowly. A few words can function as both adverbs and adjectives:
> 1. The *fast* train crashed. (adjective)
> 2. The train went *fast*. (adverb)
>
> C. Nouns often function as adverbs:
>
> Yesterday Sara fell down.
>
> In the sentence above *yesterday* names a thing, a certain day. It also tells when an action took place, so it is a noun functioning as an adverb.
>
> D. *Not* and *never* are always adverbs. They both give negative information: *not* tells how something is done (not at all) and *never* tells when something is done (not ever).

Now that you've been introduced to the adverb, see if you can underline the adverbs in the sentences below:

1. Mary and Bill swiftly and correctly named the specimen.
2. The entire class recently went away.
3. Usually we go quietly to lunch.
4. Today we did not go quietly.

ADVERB EXERCISES

A. *Directions:* Change the words listed below into adverbs. Write the adverbs in the spaces provided.

EXAMPLE: sure   surely

1. new _____
2. immediate _____
3. late _____
4. accident _____
5. able _____
6. beautiful _____
7. mystery _____
8. happy _____
9. admirable _____
10. noisy _____
11. irritable _____
12. sensible _____
13. ready _____
14. complete _____
15. shy _____
16. casual _____
17. heavy _____
18. necessary _____
19. true _____
20. intentional _____

B. *Directions:* Use *all* the adverbs listed below and write fifteen sentences. Each sentence should have at least one adverb in it. Some sentences will have more than one.

EXAMPLE: yesterday   quickly
Yesterday the giraffe quickly ate all the leaves off the tree.

swiftly	daily	almost	never	really
correctly	up	not	well	yesterday
tenderly	very	today	almost	courageously
promptly	usually	here	there	loudly

_____

_____

_____

_____

_____

_____

_____

_____

_____

_____

_____

_____

_____

_____

_____

_____

_____

_____

_____

_____

_____

_____

C. *Directions:* In the following sentences underline each adverb and write *adv.* above it.

                                           adv.
    EXAMPLE: The events in this exercise <u>really</u> happened.

THE BLACK DEATH

1. Sometimes an event can unexpectedly change the course of history.

2. In the fourteenth century the Black Death dramatically changed European society.

3. This plague killed approximately one third of Europe's population in four years.

4. A tiny bacterium, always found in the stomach of fleas, caused this disease.

5. Small animals usually carried the fleas.

6. Black rats especially carried these small insects.

7. Italian merchants unknowingly brought the plague to Europe from Asia.

8. European merchants and travelers very quickly spread the disease everywhere.

9. City streets were almost deserted.

10. Prices soared, shops closed, and necessities became extremely scarce.

11. In Paris the plague, at its peak, supposedly killed eight hundred people daily.

12. Death was very common.

13. One witness said, ". . . a dead man was then of no more account than a dead goat would be today."

14. During the plague, doctors did not know the cause of the disease.

15. They even blamed the stars, infected winds, and bad smells.

16. After the plague, Europe was never the same.

17. European society was drastically changed.

18. Europeans related to each other differently.

19. The plague also changed European governments forever.

20. Many historians have always considered the Black Death a major turning point in Europe's history.

D. *Directions:* Write a sentence to follow each of the sentence patterns given below. Use articles (*a, an, the*) wherever you need them.

EXAMPLE: ADJ   N   V

The little bird tweeted.

1. N   V   ADV

_____

2. ADJ   N   V   ADV

_____

3. ADJ   N   V   ADV

_____

4. ADJ   N   ADV   V

_____

5. ADJ   N   ADV   V   ADV

_____

6. ADV   ADJ   N   ADV   V   ADV

_____

15. PREPOSITIONS

Read the groups of words (phrases) listed below and answer the questions in the spaces provided.

A. *with the blue high-top sneakers*
    1. What is the first word in the phrase? __With__
    2. What is the last word in the phrase? __Sneakers__
    3. What part of speech is the last word? __noun__
    4. Write a sentence in which you use the phrase.

    _____

B. *after the campfire*
    1. What is the first word in the phrase? __After__
    2. What is the last word in the phrase? __camp fire__
    3. What part of speech is the last word? __noun__
    4. Write a sentence in which you use the phrase.

    _____

C. *like a chipmunk*
    1. What is the first word in the phrase? __like__
    2. What is the last word in the phrase? __chipmunk__
    3. What part of speech is the last word? __noun__
    4. Write a sentence in which you use the phrase.

    _____

What do the words *chipmunk*, *campfire*, and *sneakers* have in common? They're all nouns. The first words in the phrase (*like*, *after*, and *with*) also have something in common. They're all **prepositions**.

Definition
A **preposition** is a word that shows a relationship between a noun or pronoun and some other word in the sentence.

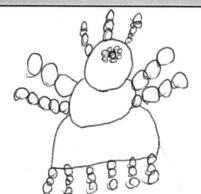

58

Look at the sentences you wrote. In each case, the preposition connects the noun following it with another word that you included in the sentence. For example:

The basketball player with the blue high-top sneakers played defense.

In the above sentence the preposition *with* connects *sneakers* to *player*. Now look again at the sentences you wrote. What two words do the prepositions in each of these sentences connect? List these words in the appropriate space below:

A. _____

B. _____

C. _____

> **Definition**
> A **prepositional phrase** always begins with a preposition and ends with a noun or a pronoun. Like any phrase, it is a group of related words that does *not* contain a subject and verb and does *not* express a complete thought.

In the next grammar book in this series, you will learn more about the prepositional phrase.

Listed below are the most commonly used prepositions. In order to recognize a preposition in a sentence, it would probably help to memorize this list. The list is in four alphabetized, evenly divided columns to make them easier to memorize.

about	below	from	throughout
above	beneath	in	to
across	beside	into	toward
after	besides	like	under
against	between	near	underneath
along	beyond	of	until
amid	but (meaning except)	off	unto
among	by	on	up
around	down	over	upon
at	during	past	with
before	except	since	within
behind	for	through	without

Sometimes a preposition may be a group of words:

on account of   in spite of
because of   instead of
according to   out of

Many prepositions can also function as adverbs:

The balloon went *up*.

In this sentence the word *up* answers the question *went, where* and, thus, functions as an adverb. If *up* were a preposition, it would be followed by a noun or pronoun:

The balloon went *up* the *tree*.

HINT   A preposition is always found at the *beginning* of a *phrase*, with a *noun* or *pronoun* at the *end* of the phrase:

The ants live *beside* the soap *dish*.

PREPOSITION EXERCISES

A. *Directions:* Underline the prepositions in the following sentences. There can be more than one preposition in each sentence.
EXAMPLE: <u>Around</u> the rock the rascal <u>with</u> the purple patches ran.

1. <u>Underneath</u> the porch the black spiders make huge webs.
2. The small child toddled <u>toward</u> the cookie.
3. The car travelled <u>past</u> the diner.
4. Everyone <u>but</u> Henry carried an instrument.
5. "<u>On</u> the signal, get ready to go," yelled the stern referee. "If you move <u>off</u> your mark, you will be disqualified."
6. <u>Among</u> the trees <u>in</u> the garden, I found the rose <u>with</u> the crimson petals.
7. Many <u>of</u> the hockey players skated <u>without</u> helmets.
8. <u>Over</u> the river and <u>through</u> the woods <u>to</u> grandmother's house we go.
9. There are several warty toads <u>between</u> the rocks <u>near</u> the pond.
10. Will you come to work <u>before</u> school or <u>after</u> classes?

B. *Directions:* Underline the prepositions in the following sentences. There can be more than one preposition in each sentence.
EXAMPLE: The ball rolled <u>into</u> the street.

1. <u>Without</u> helium the balloon will not go <u>above</u> the trees and <u>into</u> the sky.

2. At dawn the weary student finally finished his essay about the life cycle of the common cheese whizzie.
3. Fifteen students will stay in the library until Tuesday to break the All-School Library Sitting Record.
4. Who would want to sit amid all those books, away from pizza and cheeseburgers?
5. No one except those with a dedication beyond my comprehension.
6. At midnight we should go into the library and see these devoted students.
7. Like sentries at their posts, these students always remain awake and alert.
8. Throughout history their fame will spread.
9. "By Jove," Mrs. Fezziwig said. "During the dance you were behind me the entire time, Mr. Fezziwig. Now stay beside me."
10. "Upon my word," replied Mr. Fezziwig. "I will, my dear. This is the best party since the last one."

C. *Directions:* Underline the prepositions in the following sentences. There can be more than one preposition in each sentence.

EXAMPLE: The students stayed <u>for</u> the movie.

TICKET TO FREEDOM

1. Before the Civil War a group of blacks and whites in the North established the Underground Railroad.
2. They used the railroad term *station* for a hiding place and the term *conductor* for men and women helpers.
3. One of the most famous conductors of the Underground Railroad was Harriet Tubman, a former slave.
4. She made nineteen trips into the South during the 1850s and helped more than 300 slaves escape.
5. Most of the people who operated the Underground Railroad were free blacks from the North.
6. Some individual whites provided runaways with food, clothing, directions, and places to hide.
7. Most slaves escaped by themselves without anyone's help.
8. More than 75,000 slaves received help from the Underground Railroad before 1863.
9. This figure was only a small fraction of the total number of blacks in captivity.
10. Abraham Lincoln's Emancipation Proclamation set the majority of blacks free during the Civil War.

D. *Directions:* Use the following combinations of prepositions and prepositional phrases in sentences.

EXAMPLE: to   without her mother

Myra went to the train station without her mother.

1. since   without a computer

_____

2. like   beside the railroad tracks

_____

3. among   into the dark closet

_____

4. below   about the strange bubbles

_____

5. across   near the tattooed lady

_____

6. under   around the race track

_____

7. down   beneath the icy pond

_____

E. *Directions:* Put parentheses around each prepositional phrase. Underline the preposition in each phrase.

EXAMPLE: Myra went (<u>to</u> the train station) (<u>without</u> her mother.)

1. Sneezy, Grumpy, and Doc went below into the mines and returned with jewels.
2. I wanted to go to the game, but my friends wanted to stay at home.
3. Jake stayed at the club until dinner time.
4. Before class meet me behind the lockers.
5. For the past week Sarah has come to class without her book.

16. INTERJECTIONS

Hurrah! We are almost finished with this book.

How does the writer feel about almost finishing this book? Sad? Angry? Happy? Yes, probably like you, the writer feels happy. What word conveyed the emotion the writer felt? *Hurrah*, of course. Some words (like *wow, gosh, darn,* and all swear words) just express feeling and have no other job in the sentence.

> **Definition**
> Words that express sudden emotion and have no grammatical relation to other words in a sentence are called **interjections**. They are interjected—or put into—the sentence.

Because they have no relationship with the other words in the sentence, interjections are sometimes used alone. For example, people often say "Wow!" or "Darn!" in conversation and assume the listener will know what they are talking about.

Notice that each of the previous interjections has an exclamation point after it. Because it has no relationship with the rest of the sentence, an interjection always has some form of punctuation, either a comma or an exclamation point, following it. If an interjection expresses very strong emotion like "Hurrah!" or "Ouch!" it is followed by an exclamation point and sometimes a new sentence. If an interjection expresses less strong feelings like "Gee whiz," it is followed by a comma and the rest of the sentence:

1. *Ouch!* I stubbed my toe!
2. *Gee whiz,* that sunlight is bright.

As sentence 2 shows, interjections sometimes consist of two or more words:

1. *Dear me,* I forgot the kangaroo.
2. "*Oh, no!*" she cried. "I lost my history notes!"

HINT

A. An interjection usually comes at the beginning of a sentence.

B. An interjection must be followed by either a comma or an exclamation point.

For practice, underline the interjection in each of the following sentences:

1. Wow! This gift is exactly what I wanted.
2. Eureka! Henry decoded the cryptogram.
3. Oh, I thought you didn't want the last piece of cake, so I ate it.

INTERJECTION EXERCISES

A. *Directions:* Underline each interjection.

EXAMPLE: <u>Gee</u>, I didn't come up with the same answer.

1. Oh, no! I forgot to study for the test!
2. Well, there's no way I'm ever going to pass this one.
3. Hey, why don't they ever ask something I know?
4. Ouch! All this writing is hurting my hand.
5. Oops! My pen just leaked all over my paper.
6. Oh well, that answer was wrong anyway.
7. Aha! I just figured out what the question means.
8. Phooey, I can't remember the answer.
9. Horrors! Time is up, and I just got started.
10. Whew, am I glad that's over.

B. *Directions:* Using either the interjections listed below or others that you know, write a sentence for each of the following situations.

EXAMPLE: You are surprised that a friend has a motorcycle.
<u>By Jove! I didn't know you rode a motorcycle.</u>

whew	ouch	help
hurry	my goodness	alas
ah	oh	tsk, tsk
zounds	wow	dear me
eek	aha	eureka
all right	darn	oh, no
shoot	gee whiz	ah me

1. You are relieved that you passed the examination.

   _____

2. You are somewhat surprised that you finished your homework early.

   _____

3. You are disappointed that your favorite program is not on T.V.

   _____

4. You are having difficulty with your homework.

   _____

5. You have just received your report card.

   _____

6. You have just won an important game.

   _____

7. Your pet has run away.

   _____

8. You just found the homework that you thought you had lost.

   _____

9. You have just discovered that you do not have the homework that you thought you had put in your notebook.

   _____

10. You are confused about what the teacher covered in English class today, and your homework is on today's lesson.

    _____

17. CONJUNCTIONS

COORDINATING CONJUNCTIONS

To find out more about conjunctions, read the following sentences and answer the questions in the spaces provided.

A. She was tired and sore.
   1. What words are the adjectives? _tired, sore_
   2. What word joins the adjectives? _was_
B. The dog Sounder limped but moved joyfully toward his master.
   1. What words are the verbs? _limped mooved toward_
   2. What word joins the verbs? _____
C. Sherry or Pat will conduct the meeting after school and take the minutes.
   1. What words are the verbs? _meeting   take_
   2. What word joins the verbs? _the_
   3. What words are the subjects? _Sherry, Pat_
   4. What word joins the subjects? _or_

What words join other words in the above sentences? *And, but,* and *or.* Which words are the conjunctions? Again, *and, but,* and *or.* **Conjunctions** are words that join.

There are three types of conjunctions: **coordinating, correlative,** and **subordinating.** We will study only the first two in this lesson. The conjunctions above are called **coordinating conjunctions.** Can you tell why they are called *coordinating* conjunctions?

Definition
Coordinating conjunctions join words or groups of words of equal rank. For now, the term equal rank means words of the same part of speech or function.

Look at sentences A, B, and C above. Adjective is joined with adjective, verb with verb, and noun with noun. In a later lesson you will see how a simple sentence can be joined with another simple sentence.

There are only six coordinating conjunctions: *for, and, nor, but, or,* and *yet*. They are easy to remember. Notice how the first letter of each spells the word *fanboy*.

> For
> And
> Nor
> But
> Or
> Yet

CORRELATIVE CONJUNCTIONS

There is another kind of conjunction. See what you can find out about it from the sentences below. Read the sentences and answer the questions in the spaces provided.

A. Neither Jill nor Jack will be taking the final examination in the head–trauma course.
   1. What words are the subjects? _Jill   Jack_
   2. What words are joining the subjects? _Neither nor_

B. Amy not only sang during the concert but also played the piano.
   1. What words are the verbs? _sang   played_
   2. What words join the verbs? _but also   not only_

> **Definition**
> The conjunctions in the above sentences are pairs of words: *neither . . . nor* and *not only . . . but also*. Conjunctions in pairs are called **correlative conjunctions**. Like many relatives (*correlative*), they choose not to stand alone.

There are five pairs of correlative conjunctions:

> neither . . . nor
> either . . . or
> both . . . and
> not only . . . but (also)
> whether . . . or

Like the coordinating conjunction, the correlative conjunction joins words or groups of words of equal rank.

For practice, underline the coordinating and correlative conjunctions in the sentences below. Remember, correlative conjunctions must be used in pairs. Write the kind of conjunction above each one.

1. The committee cannot decide whether to buy a VCR or to rent one.
2. After the performance, she was exhausted but satisfied.
3. Horace sent invitations to both the sixth and seventh grades.
4. Marty and Pat were absent yesterday but took the test anyhow.

HINT   *For* can be a preposition as well as a coordinating conjunction:

I made the cake *for* her. (preposition)
She was proud, *for* she had finished the marathon. (coordinating conjunction)

Yet can be an adverb as well as a coordinating conjunction:

Uncle Conrad hasn't arrived yet. (adverb)
The baby was fussy, yet cute. (coordinating conjunction)

CONJUNCTION EXERCISES

A. *Directions:* Underline each conjunction in the following sentences. Write *coor.* above each coordinating conjunction and *corl.* over each correlative conjunction.

EXAMPLE: Either you or I should call or write our grandfather.

WOMEN'S STRUGGLE FOR THE VOTE

1. At one time women could neither vote nor enjoy other political or economic rights.
2. In 1848 Elizabeth Cady Stanton and Lucretia Mott organized a convention on women's rights.
3. As a child, Elizabeth Cady Stanton had heard women complain about men who legally squandered their wives' earnings on liquor or sold their wives' earnings without consent.
4. As women, Elizabeth Cady Stanton and Lucretia Mott could attend an anti-slavery meeting but could not participate.
5. Stanton and Mott saw these injustices and decided to hold a convention at Seneca Falls, New York.
6. Both men and women attended the convention.

7. Before the convention, neither Stanton's husband nor her friends supported giving women the right to vote.

8. In her speech at the meeting, Stanton said that only women could win equal rights, for they alone could understand the injustices.

9. The convention both signed a formal "Declaration of Sentiments" and passed a resolution demanding the right to vote for women.

10. The public's reaction to the women who supported the resolution was either to ridicule them or to attack them viciously.

11. The formal "Declaration of Sentiments" not only copied the Declaration of Independence in style and language but also declared women's independence from men.

12. The fight for the women's vote was long and hard, yet the courageous actions of women like Stanton and Mott eventually achieved victory.

13. In 1920 women voted for the first time, and Charlotte Woodard, the only surviving female participant of the Seneca Falls Convention, was among them.

B. *Directions:* Read the following sentences. Use either a coordinating conjunction or correlative conjunction to make each pair or group of sentences into one sentence. Keep the original meaning as much as possible.

EXAMPLE: Mandy rode her bike one day. She rode her skateboard the next.

Mandy rode her bike one day and her skateboard the next day.

1. Bill will go to the dance. Jeff will go to the dance. Winifred will go to the dance.

bill will go to the dance and Jeff will go to the dance
and winifred will go to the dance

2. King Arthur loved Guinevere. Lancelot loved Guinevere.

King arthur loved Guinever and Lancelot loved Guinevere

3. Demeter did not want to give up Persephone. Hades, god of the underworld, did not want to give her up either.

Demeter did not want to give up persephone but
Hades the god of the under world did not want
give her up either

4. Greedy Midas loved gold. He also loved his daughter.

Greed Midas loved gold and his daughter

5. Echo wanted to talk to Narcissus. She could only repeat what he said.

Echo wanted to talk to Narcissus but could only repeat what he said

6. Many people do not want to use nuclear energy. They also do not want to use solar energy.

Many people do not want to use nuclear energy but don't want to use solar energy

7. Deborah would make a good president. Peter would make a good president.

Deborah would make a good president Peter also would make a good president

8. Zenobia must choose a pet. She can choose a cat. She can choose a dog.

Zenobia must choose not only dose she want a cat but also wants a dog

9. Helen of Troy was the most beautiful woman in the ancient world. It was her face that "launched a thousand ships."

Helen of Troy was the most beautiful woman in the ancient world and it was her face that "launched a thousand ships

10. Sarah gave each person a card. She gave each person a present.

Sarah gave each person a card and a present

C. *Directions:* Read the following sentences. Use either a coordinating conjunction or correlative conjunction to make each pair or group of sentences into one sentence. Keep the original meaning as much as possible.

EXAMPLE: Ruby likes movies. Roy likes movies, too.
Both Ruby and Roy like movies.

1. Will you walk the dog now? Will you walk the dog later?

Will you walk the dog now or later

2. James had not cleaned his room. James had not completed his homework.

James had not cleaned his room or completed his homework

3. Go to the store. Buy two quarts of milk, one dozen eggs, and a pound of rice.

Go to the store and buy 2 quarts of milk one dozen eggs and a pound of rice

4. On Tuesday Marion walked to school. On Friday her father drove her.

On tuesday marion walked to school but on Friday her father drove her

5. The manager hired Jill. She was qualified for the job.

The manager hired Jill for she was qualified for the job.

6. Have the flowers arrived yet? Have the balloons arrived?

Have the flowers and balloons arrived Yet

7. Christopher Columbus set sail to find Asia. He discovered America.

Christopher Columbus set sail to find Asia but discovered America

8. We will travel to Washington, D.C. We will visit Williamsburg, too.

We will travel to Washington, D.C. and visit Williamsburg too

9. Doctor Watson thought Sherlock Holmes was dead. Sherlock Holmes returned to solve more crimes. Sherlock Holmes continued to pursue Professor Moriarty.

Doctor Watson thought Sherlock Holmes was dead but Sherlock Holmes returned to solve more crime and continued to pursue Professor Moriarty

10. Mortimer hadn't cleaned out his locker. Janet hadn't cleaned out hers.

Mortimer hadn't cleaned out his locker and neither had Janet

D. *Directions:* Write a sentence to follow each pattern given below. You may use articles wherever you need them. You may use either type of conjunction for CONJ.

EXAMPLE: S   V   CONJ   ADJ   CONJ   ADJ
She is not only strong but fast.

1. ADJ   CONJ   ADJ   S   V.

_____

2. ADJ   CONJ   ADJ   S   CONJ   S   V.

_____

3. ADJ   CONJ   ADJ   S   CONJ   S   V   CONJ   V.

_____

4. ADJ CONJ ADJ S CONJ S V CONJ V ADV CONJ ADV.

_____

5. INT   ADJ   CONJ   ADJ   S   CONJ   S   V   CONJ   V.

_____

6. CONJ   S   CONJ   S   V.

_____

7. S   CONJ   V   CONJ   V.

_____

18. COMPOUNDS

With conjunctions you can write more interesting and informative sentences. Many sentences together made up of ones—one subject, one verb, one adjective, and so on—would be boring at best. With a conjunction you can join (make **compound**) words or sentences.

This section explains three types of compounds: **compound subjects, compound verbs,** and **compound sentences.**

COMPOUND SUBJECTS

Read the following sentences and answer the questions in the spaces provided.

A. Tom and Jerry chased each other throughout the house.

    1. What word is the verb? _____

    2. What words are the subjects? _____

    3. What word joins the subjects? _____

B. Either Sakeena, Kim, or Juan will give the speech.

    1. What is the verb phrase? _____

    2. What words are the subjects? _____

    3. What *words* join the subjects? _____

C. In Greek mythology Zeus, Hades, and Poseidon were brothers.

    1. What word is the verb? _____

    2. What words are the subjects? _____

    3. What word joins the subjects? _____

In the sentences above, more than one subject is present. These subjects are joined by a conjunction. In the first sentence, *and* joins *Tom* and *Jerry*. In the second sentence, *either . . . or* joins *Sakeena, Kim,* and *Juan*, and in the third sentence *and* joins *Zeus, Hades,* and *Poseidon*. Subjects joined by a conjunction become a compound subject.

> **Definition**
> A **compound subject** is two or more subjects that are joined by a conjunction (either *coordinating* or *correlative*) and share the same verb or verbs.

Now underline the compound subject in the sentence below:

My aunt and uncle have taken care of me since I was two.

COMPOUND VERBS

Remember, a writer can also join two or more verbs with a conjunction. In the following sentences underline the subjects once and the verbs twice. Label the conjunctions *coor.* for coordinating and *corl.* for correlative.

1. Wilma both sang and danced at the party.

2. The girls' sports class will do warm-up exercises and then play softball.

Notice that the subject in each sentence is doing the action of two verbs. *Wilma* does the action of the verbs *sang* and *danced*, and *class* does the action of *do* and *play*. What words join the verbs in each sentence? Again, conjunctions: *both . . . and* in the first sentence; *and* in the second sentence. Verbs joined by a conjunction become a **compound verb**.

> **Definition**
> A **compound verb** is two or more verbs that are joined by a conjunction and share the same subject or subjects.

For practice, underline the conjunctions in each sentence. Put parentheses around the words that each conjunction joins and label them:

1. Harriet not only washed the car but also waxed it.

2. Neither Saul nor Chip had seen the movie before.

3. Myra and Sally came home early from the party and went to sleep.

4. Jean, Sam, and Dennis decided to adopt the skinny dog.

COMPOUND SENTENCES

Use a coordinating conjunction to make one sentence out of each pair of sentences listed below. A comma must be placed before the coordinating conjunction that you add.

1. In the race the motorcycle had the lead. The sports car soon passed it.

2. Mrs. Valdez was happy. She had just created the world's largest anchovy pizza.

_____

3. The delivery man dropped off the package at the store. The storekeeper unwrapped it.

_____

You have just turned six simple sentences into three **compound sentences**.

> **Definition**
> Two or more simple sentences (independent clauses) joined by a coordinating conjunction are called a **compound sentence**.

As you've learned already, an independent clause is another name for a simple sentence: it can stand by itself, be independent, and make sense.

When you join simple sentences with conjunctions, you create more interesting sentences. Compound sentences break up the boredom of one simple sentence after another and another followed by another and so on throughout a paragraph or story.

In a compound sentence you can show more precisely how one idea relates to another by using the conjunction that best expresses the relationship between these ideas. Look again at the sentences at the beginning of this section. You'll find that some conjunctions make the meaning clearer than others.

The motorcycle had the lead in the race, but the sports car soon passed it.

The sentence above makes more sense than:

The motorcycle had the lead in the race, and the sports car soon passed it.

The first rewrite shows the surprise of the action. When you read about the action in the first part, you don't expect the action of the second part. _But_ and _yet_ are coordinating conjunctions that emphasize the unexpected or contrast the different. The conjunction _and_ merely joins the two sentences as if they were equal in excitement. The second rewrite makes the action sound commonplace and humdrum.

Sentence 2 above needs a conjunction which expresses another kind of relationship. One sentence caused the action of the other sentence. Can you tell which sentence caused the action of the other? If Mrs. Valdez hadn't made the world's largest anchovy pizza, would she be happy? The action of the second sentence caused the response told in the first sentence. In the compound sentence below, the coordinating conjunction *for* tells the reader that one part of the compound sentence causes the other part:

Mrs. Valdez was happy, for she had made the world's largest anchovy pizza.

Other conjunctions express other relationships:

Conjunction	Relationship	Example
either . . . or	choice	*Either* you buy it, *or* I will.
or	choice	Would you prefer turkey *or* fish?
both . . . and	joining	*Both* Judy *and* Zia hate the winter.
and	joining	Tracy swam *and* danced all summer.
not only . . . but also	joining	Rex *not only* lost his shoes, *but also* lost his socks.
for	cause and effect	Jose hesitated, *for* he had never eaten snails before.
yet	contrast	Ruth didn't want to go, *yet* she didn't want to hurt Don's feelings.
but	contrast	Sid visited France, *but* he didn't like it.

HINT

1. A comma must be placed before a coordinating conjunction in a compound sentence.
   EXAMPLE: Vera swept the hall, and Billy washed the windows.

2. Different conjunctions express different relationships.

COMPOUND EXERCISES

A. *Directions:* In the following sentences change the plural subjects to compound subjects. Try using three or more subjects in some sentences.

EXAMPLE: They went early to the concert to obtain good seats.
James, Janine, and Jerry went early to the concert to obtain good seats.

1. We went to the game early to set up the refreshment stand.

_____

2. The teams had early practices and then discussed strategy for the next day's games.

_____

3. Spring flowers always bring thoughts of summer vacation.

_____

4. They desperately wanted to go on a three-day canoe trip on the Allagash with their friends.

_____

5. The musical groups appeared in the stadium for the benefit concert.

_____

6. The dogs barked loudly, and Ms. Winter quickly let them out.

_____

7. Some cars need frequent tune-ups, but others can go for months without one.

_____

8. Holidays are more than welcome to all students.

_____

9. Authors write so readers can understand the characters and perhaps understand themselves better.

_____

10. Birds make good pets for people who like to change newspapers, but fish are quieter.

_____

11. Radio stations often play only a few songs from an album, and they play them over and over.

_____

12. Today's movies sometimes comment on life as well as offer entertainment.

_____

13. Many sports are shown on T.V.

_____

14. His clothing was wrinkled, and his shoes were untied. (What other change must you make in this sentence?)

_____

15. The jury has voted to order pizza with pepperoni but without mushrooms. (What other change must you make in this sentence?)

_____

B. *Directions:* In the following sentences insert a compound verb in the spaces provided.
EXAMPLE: The wolf <u>huffed and puffed</u> but it did no good.

1. Everyone _____ at the party.
2. In the movie all of the actors _____.
3. Scout, Jem, and Dill _____ all summer long.
4. Teachers always _____.
5. When catching a unicorn, make sure you not only _____ but also _____.
6. Friends should _____ thoughtfully but shouldn't _____.
7. The detective will either _____ or _____.
8. During the game, the fans _____.
9. After the heavy rains, the rivers and streams _____.
10. Before a test, I _____.

C. *Directions:* Read the following sentences. Underline the compound subjects once and the compound verbs twice.
EXAMPLE: The windows <u>rattled and banged</u> in the wind.

ACHIEVEMENTS OF EARLY LATIN AMERICAN INDIANS

1. In the 1500s Spanish explorers invaded and conquered the Indian tribes of Latin America.
2. European rulers and clergy believed that the Indian societies were primitive, uncivilized, and inferior.
3. In truth, the Mayans, Aztecs, and Incas often surpassed the Europeans in many areas.

4. Mayan mathematicians invented and used a superior mathematical system.
5. Their discovery and use of the zero allowed them to calculate into the millions.
6. The Mayans and Aztecs developed a 365-day calendar.
7. Neither the French nor the Spanish had developed a more accurate calendar.
8. The population and size of the Aztec capital was substantially larger than any Spanish city of its day.
9. The Aztecs of Mexico and the Incas of Peru ruled empires larger than most European states.
10. Over 60,000 visitors shopped daily and browsed in the shops of the Aztec capital.
11. The palace of the Aztec emperor had three hundred rooms and was larger than the palace of the French king.
12. The dry climate and steep terrain of the Incan empire did not prevent growing enough food to feed its 12,000,000 inhabitants.
13. The technique of terraced farming and a network of irrigation canals made Incan farmers as advanced as farmers anywhere in Europe.

D. *Directions:* Read the following sentences. Use a conjunction to make each pair of simple sentences into a compound sentence. Use the conjunction that makes the best relationship between the sentences. Don't forget to use a comma before a coordinating conjunction in a compound sentence.

EXAMPLE: The cat can run very fast. The dog can run faster.
      The cat can run very fast, but the dog can run faster.

AN AMERICAN LEGEND

1. Folk stories often reveal much about a country. American tall tales are no exception.

_____

2. Our tall tales reveal the constant movement of our pioneer forefathers. They also reveal valued human characteristics.

_____

3. Paul Bunyan is a famous American folk hero. He was born in Nova Scotia, Canada.

_____

4. His parents were French fisherfolk. His name was originally Paul Bonjean.

_____

5. At birth Paul weighed over fifty pounds. All the cows in the neighborhood gave their milk for Paul's food.

_____

6. His parents were very worried. Paul outgrew everything.

_____

7. His clothes did not fit. His cradle did not fit.

_____

8. An unused mainsail became his diapers. The largest ship's hull in the China trade became his cradle.

_____

9. Paul was extremely bright. He had problems in school.

_____

10. He could fit only one letter on each page. His geography book had to be carried by a team of oxen.

_____

11. One day he accidentally sat on his lunch box. When he opened it, he discovered his first invention, hamburger.

_____

12. Paul left school. He had to choose his career.

_____

13. He tried fishing, hunting, and trapping. They were too easy.

_____

14. He retreated to a cave. There he met his lifelong companion, Babe.

_____

15. Babe, an ox as big as Paul, was a very strange shade of blue. As a calf she had been abandoned in the deepest snow on record and had never lost the color of that deep chill.

_____

16. One day Babe knocked down a tree. Then Paul knew he was to invent logging to clear the land for American pioneers.

_____

17. Nothing could stop Paul. Thirst did not stop him. Heat did not stop him.

_____

18. When Babe was thirsty, Paul dug a drinking hole that is now the famous geyser, Old Faithful. When Paul became hot, he walked in a river and made the Grand Canyon.

_____

19. This ingenious American folk hero was bigger than life. American settlers saw their new land as endless and wanted to be as creative and sturdy as Paul Bunyan.

_____

E. *Directions:* Underline each conjunction in the following sentences and put parentheses around the items it joins. Label the items *s* for subject, *v* for verb, or *sen.* for sentence.

EXAMPLE: Jules and Jim went swimming.

(Jules)ˢ and (Jim)ˢ went swimming.

1. Nancy took a shower and washed her hair.
2. Bob Cratchit looked forward to Christmas and celebrated with much glee.
3. In summer, students rest from schoolwork and participate in other activities.
4. Superman is a traditional hero in many ways, but he was born in outer space.
5. Were either you or Isabel at the game last night?
6. At the zoo we saw many animals but liked the panda most.
7. Margaret Mitchell is best known for her book *Gone with the Wind*, for she wrote no other novels.
8. Bilbo, Gandalf, and twelve dwarfs went off to slay the dragon.
9. Anne Frank was killed in a Nazi concentration camp during World War II, but her spirit lives on in her diary.
10. The clean-up committee will take down the decorations, put away the chairs, and wash the floor.

F. *Directions:* Underline each conjunction in the following sentences and put parentheses around the items it joins. Label the items *s* for subject, *v* for verb, or *sen.* for sentence.

EXAMPLE: Rory (ran) to town <u>and</u> (bought) a shirt.

1. Both the teachers and the librarians suggested good books to the class.

2. No one recommended *Death Be Not Proud*, yet I found it hard to put down.

3. Myra read *To Kill a Mockingbird* and especially liked the surprise ending.

4. Many students enjoyed the rebellious Huck Finn and then read *The Adventures of Tom Sawyer*.

5. Sam and his brother like animal stories.

6. Sam is reading *Sounder*, and his brother is reading *The Incredible Journey*.

7. Many of us read books recently published, yet others picked up books published a long time ago.

8. The teachers like us to read old-fashioned books, but we sometimes like to read books about teenagers today.

9. Many books tell about teenagers today and help us understand ourselves better.

10. There are many novels and short stories about teen-agers in the Young Adult section in the library.

19. SUBJECT AND VERB AGREEMENT

Read the following sentences. Find the error in each one. Correct the error in the space provided.

1. The songs contains many harmonious guitar parts.

_____

2. My father have shown me how to throw a curve ball.

_____

3. Both Ms. Peabody's class and Mr. Wong's class eats lunch at noon and then goes to music class.

_____

These sentences don't sound right. Your ear probably hears the errors even if you don't know the name for them. What parts don't fit together? If you're having trouble finding the errors, go back and underline each verb twice and each subject once. What do you discover?

In the first sentence the subject mentions more than one song (*songs*) but the verb, *contains*, is singular.

In the second sentence the subject, *father*, is singular, but the verb, *have shown*, is plural.

In the last sentence there are two subjects, *Ms. Peabody's class* and *Mr. Wong's class*, joined by a coordinating conjunction. Like an addition sign (+), a coordinating conjunction adds these two subjects together to make a plural. The error? Each verb, *eats* and *goes*, is singular.

Definition
A verb must **agree** with its subject in number. If the subject is singular, the verb must be singular. If the subject is plural, then the verb must be plural.

The two chickens have decided not to lay eggs.

The farmer has decided to serve roast chicken.

In the sentences above, the plural subject, *chickens*, takes a plural verb, *have decided*, while the singular subject, *farmer*, takes a singular verb, *has decided*.

Subjects and verbs must agree in other ways that your ear can also probably hear. In later grammar books you will study other forms of agreement.

A. If a compound subject is joined by *and*, the verb is plural. Remember, the *and* acts as an addition sign:

Jean and Ed are cousins.

B. If the compound verb is joined by *or* or *nor*, the verb agrees with the nearest subject:
   1. Neither the coach nor the *players think* the team will lose.
   2. Neither the players nor the *coach thinks* the team will lose.
   3. Neither he nor *I am* ready for the audition.

C. Be careful not to confuse the subject of a sentence with the noun or pronoun that follows a preposition:
   1. One of these stories *is* a lie. (**not** *are*)
   2. The ears on that rabbit *are* huge. (**not** *is*)

For practice, write the correct verb for each subject in the space provided:

1. The picture (hangs, hang) on the first floor of the   _____
   museum.
2. The picture of the cottages (hangs, hang) on the   _____
   first floor of the museum.
3. The bird watchers quietly (stalks, stalk) the gray-   _____
   tipped chalk eater.
4. Either my father or brothers (has packed, have   _____
   packed) my lunch.

SUBJECT AND VERB AGREEMENT EXERCISES

A. *Directions:* Some verbs and subjects are listed below. For each verb write a subject in the space provided that agrees with the verb. For each subject write a verb in the space provided that agrees with the subject.
   EXAMPLE: walks ____*Jerry*____
            birds ____*fly*____

   1. Henry and Terry _____

   2. _____ doesn't

   3. Many of the people _____

4. Either the blue or the gray one _____

5. _____ crept

6. oxen _____

7. class _____

8. participants _____

9. _____ go

10. Either you or they _____

B. *Directions*: Some verbs and subjects are listed below. For each verb write a subject in the space provided that agrees with the verb. For each subject write a verb in the space provided that agrees with the subject.

EXAMPLE: had seen __*many lifeguards*__

1. _____ don't

2. _____ have been

3. sheep _____

4. _____ were

5. women _____

6. Either the club members or the president _____

7. Several dancers _____

8. Neither the team nor the spectators _____

9. _____ am

10. Both you and I _____

C. *Directions:* Circle the correct verb in the parentheses.
EXAMPLE: Several boys (has tried, (have tried)) out for the team.

MYSTERIOUS MONSTER

1. Many people in the United States and Canada (believes / believe) in the existence of Bigfoot.
2. Some Indian tribes (calls / call) this apelike creature Sasquatch.
3. One hundred and fifty years ago, the first report of a "wild man" (was / were) published in a New Orleans newspaper.
4. Since then over one thousand sightings of Bigfoot (has / have) been reported.
5. Each one of these reports (describes / describe) a large, furry creature of some sort with broad shoulders and long arms.
6. Red or glowing eyes, a strong, unpleasant odor, and an upright walk on two feet (is / are) characteristics often mentioned.

7. The height of the creature (is / are) said to range from seven to ten feet.

8. Its tracks (measures / measure) seventeen inches long and seven inches wide.

9. One of the most interesting claims of Bigfoot's existence (is / are) found in a short movie.

10. In the movie, scenes supposedly (shows / show) a female Bigfoot.

11. The blurred images and the camera's distance from the creature (makes / make) it impossible to see clearly.

12. People looking at the film (disagrees / disagree) about the subject.

13. Many people (says / say) it is a female Bigfoot, and others (says / say) it isn't.

14. A few scientists (thinks / think) that Bigfoot may be a distant relative of an apelike animal.

15. Theories (states / state) that this apelike creature migrated during prehistoric times from Asia to North America.

16. Most people, however, (remains / remain) unconvinced that Bigfoot exists.

17. Neither scientists nor anyone else (seems / seem) able to explain the many sightings of Bigfoot.

18. Maybe this creature really (does / do) exist.

19. There (is / are) no other explanations.

20. What (is / are) your thoughts about Bigfoot?

D. *Directions:* In each sentence choose the verb that agrees with the subject. Write your answer in the space provided.
   EXAMPLE: Several girls also (has tried, have tried) out. *have tried*

1. The small boy (walks, walk) to kindergarten by himself.
   _____

2. The science class (doesn't, don't) want to go to the museum by bus. _____

3. My mother and I (hasn't, haven't) seen that movie.
   _____

4. Neither Nicholas nor Katharine (has, have) left.
   _____

5. Both Doug and Mary (has been, have been) seen there.
   _____

6. Either Dan or Yoni (needs, need) extra study time.
   _____

7. People in the bus (leaves, leave) by the rear door.

_____

8. Neither you nor I (am, are) ready to audition.

_____

9. Both of us (was, were) nervous at the dance.

_____

10. My sweat pants (slips, slip) down during exercises.

_____

11. Where (has, have) all the doughnuts gone? _____

12. There (is, are) only two possible answers. _____

13. One of the cows (has, have) slipped through the fence.

_____

14. A member of the band always (helps, help) set up the equipment.

_____

15. Three of the gang (seems, seem) uninterested in the concert.

_____

16. Marilyn's overalls (was, were) covered with dirt.

_____

17. The teachers and the class (sees, see) a filmstrip once a week.

_____

18. Neither the teachers nor the class (misses, miss) the filmstrips.

_____

19. The horses in the barn (doesn't, don't) move.

_____

20. Every one of her flowers (grows, grow) large and fragrant.

_____

20. COMPREHENSIVE EXERCISES

PARTS OF SPEECH

A. *Directions:* Write the correct part of speech above each underlined word. If a noun functions as either an adjective or an adverb, label it according to its function.

N for noun	ADV for adverb
PRO for pronoun	PREP for preposition
V for verb	CONJ for conjunction
ADJ for adjective	INT for interjection

EXAMPLE: The United States Constitution changed <u>the</u> history <u>not only</u>
[ADJ]   [CONJ]
of the United States <u>but also</u> of the world.
[CONJ]

THE MAKING OF THE U.S. CONSTITUTION

1. In May, 1787, <u>fifty-five</u> delegates from twelve states met at the Constitutional Convention in Philadelphia to discuss replacing the <u>Articles of Confederation</u>.

2. The Articles of Confederation were the rules <u>of</u> government under which the colonies <u>had fought</u> the Revolutionary War.

3. These Articles brought <u>together</u> thirteen independent colonies into <u>a</u> "firm league of friendship" to fight England.

4. After the Revolutionary War, the fragile union of the colonies began to fall <u>apart</u>, and the Articles of Confederation could not hold <u>them</u> together.

5. Each state government had more <u>power</u> than the Congress, and each state felt it was more important than its neighboring states <u>or</u> even the United States itself.

6. Each state <u>could</u> make <u>its</u> own money, and some states printed so much paper money that it was almost worthless.

7. To help raise money, some states <u>taxed</u> people just for crossing the state line <u>from</u> another state.

8. In 1787 the unexpected and violent rebellion of Daniel Shays, <u>a</u> former Massachusetts captain <u>in</u> the Revolutionary Army, finally forced many leaders to review the Articles.

9. Shays <u>collected</u> an army of desperate, debt-ridden farmers to pro-test the seizure of farms, but ultimately this small group of armed men prevented the Supreme Court <u>from</u> meeting in Springfield, Massachusetts.

10. In order to prevent the <u>capture</u> of the Federal arsenal, the Congress of the United States <u>frantically</u> voted to raise money for an army.

11. <u>Alas,</u> twelve of the thirteen states ignored the request for money, and <u>finally</u> wealthy men from Massachusetts gave the money to raise the army that defeated Shays.

12. The Congress was powerless <u>not only</u> to raise money for an army against Shays, but also to collect taxes for any armed defense <u>during</u> the war.

13. Many of the <u>country's</u> leaders feared that soon thirteen indepen-dent countries <u>would exist,</u> so in 1787 many became delegates to the Constitutional Convention in Philadelphia.

14. The delegates elected George Washington as the leader of this convention, and <u>he</u> skillfully guided the <u>often</u> heated discussion.

15. <u>Throughout</u> the hot, humid summer convention delegates de-bated the value of a central government's authority versus the value of each <u>state's</u> authority.

16. Finally, on <u>September</u> 17, <u>1787,</u> all the delegates signed the Con-stitution of the United States.

17. <u>Under</u> the new Constitution the states kept some powers, <u>but</u> others were given only to the central government.

18. The Constitution created a central government <u>with</u> three equal branches: the <u>legislative,</u> the executive, and the judicial.

19. The Constitution granted power to each branch to check any of the other three branches, so <u>no</u> authority <u>had</u> all the power.

20. The Constitution of the United States established <u>for</u> the first time in history a government created by a nation's citizens and <u>not</u> by those who governed.

B. *Directions:* Write the correct part of speech above each underlined word. If a noun or pronoun functions as either an adjective or an adverb, label it according to its function.

N for noun	ADV for adverb
PRO for pronoun	PREP for preposition
V for verb	CONJ for conjunction
ADJ for adjective	INT for interjection

                    ADJ   V
EXAMPLE: The story of Daedalus and Icarus is a lesson in how to
behave.

DAEDALUS AND ICARUS: A GREEK MYTH

1. The myth of <u>Daedalus</u> and Icarus reveals the most important value of <u>ancient</u> Greek society.

2. The story begins with Daedalus, <u>an</u> extremely gifted craftsman in all <u>things</u> scientific and <u>artistic</u>.

3. Every ruler in Greece and the surrounding kingdoms wanted this <u>master's</u> services, but Daedalus desired <u>only</u> the freedom to wander.

4. One of <u>his</u> journeys brought <u>him</u> to the Mediterranean island of Crete.

5. King Minos <u>asked</u> Daedalus to plan for the king the most beautiful palace <u>ever</u> built.

6. Daedalus <u>obliged</u> the king and designed a palace <u>with</u> a fantastic labyrinth (maze) <u>underneath</u>.

7. King Minos saw the finished palace and said to Daedalus, "<u>By</u> Zeus! <u>Never</u> has such a beautiful palace <u>been seen</u> by <u>either</u> men <u>or</u> gods."

8. Daedalus lived <u>on</u> Crete, in the <u>king's</u> <u>favor</u>, until one fateful day.

9. Ariadne, King Minos's daughter, was <u>almost</u> sick with love <u>for</u> Theseus, a Greek hero trapped in the labyrinth.

10. <u>She</u> asked Daedalus how Theseus <u>might</u> escape, and Daedalus told her.

11. Theseus escaped and took <u>Adriadne</u> with <u>him</u>.

12. King Minos was angry <u>beyond</u> measure and imprisoned Daedalus and <u>his</u> son, Icarus, in the labyrinth.

13. Daedalus and Icarus <u>easily</u> escaped from the labyrinth, but how <u>were</u> they to leave the island?

14. The <u>wily</u> Daedalus built two sets of wings from feathers and wax so he <u>and</u> his son could fly <u>over</u> the sea.

15. "<u>Well,</u> my son," said Daedalus. "These wings will help to set <u>us</u> free, <u>but</u> do <u>not</u> fly close to either the sun or the sea or you <u>will</u> surely perish."

16. Icarus began their flight <u>by</u> obediently trailing his father, but the ecstasy of soaring weightlessly <u>through</u> the air proved <u>too</u> much.

17. He flew closer and <u>closer</u> to the sun, and his wings melted <u>into</u> useless lumps.

18. Cursing his own invention, grief-stricken Daedalus buried his most beloved son on the island that still <u>bears</u> his son's name.

19. Daedalus sadly went <u>on</u> his way to escape the murderous <u>anger</u> of Minos.

20. To the Greeks this story taught the lesson of <u>never</u> going <u>to</u> extremes but of doing all things in moderation.

C. *Directions:* Write the correct part of speech above each underlined word. If a noun or pronoun functions as either an adjective or an adverb, label it according to its function.

N for noun	ADV for adverb
PRO for pronoun	CONJ for conjunction
V for verb	PREP for preposition
ADJ for adjective	INT for interjection

               ADV   PREP
EXAMPLE: <u>There</u> are many types <u>of</u> sports.

1. The referee signaled a penalty of <u>fifteen</u> yards <u>for</u> holding.

2. Julius tentatively placed his foot in the only <u>toehold</u> on the <u>almost</u> sheer rock face.

3. <u>Before</u> the competition Gladys practiced <u>over</u> and over <u>her</u> figure eights, <u>for</u> she wanted to win the <u>ice</u> skating championship.

4. Bobbing almost aimlessly in the <u>white</u> water, Sabrina's canoe barely made <u>it</u> <u>through</u> the deadly rapids.

5. The baseball hit the wall <u>in</u> left <u>field</u>, but Jim quickly <u>fielded</u> it and made a double play.

6. Larry <u>had dribbled</u> the ball deftly down center court and made the basket.

7. Sweat poured <u>over</u> Jill's brow, <u>yet</u> she dug her toes <u>into</u> the cinders and placed her heels in the starting block.

8. She tried to block the kick, but the ball went <u>between</u> the <u>goalie's</u> legs.

9. During the frantic <u>pace</u> of the aerobic exercises, Jack felt his heart pounding <u>throughout</u> his body.

10. Jenna raised her stick and <u>drove</u> the ball <u>toward</u> the right wing.

11. <u>Eager</u> to show his accomplishments, Jeff <u>chalked</u> his hands and headed confidently to the parallel bars.

12. <u>Never</u> having played <u>this</u> position, Mike nervously skated <u>after</u> the puck.

13. The coxswain rhythmically chanted, and the four rowers <u>vigorously</u> rowed in <u>unison</u>.

14. Greg walked to the <u>end</u> of the diving board, poised himself on the <u>edge</u>, and <u>then</u> dove into the water.

15. <u>From</u> the top of the slope, the ski run <u>seemed</u> to stretch almost to the <u>next</u> mountain, <u>yet</u> Bob was determined to get to the <u>bottom</u>.

16. Tired beyond <u>endurance</u>, Maria turned the corner and jogged <u>home</u>.

17. <u>The</u> sail began to luff, <u>for</u> John had headed the boat <u>away</u> from the wind.

18. As the bicyclist rode <u>up</u> the hill, he <u>shifted</u> gears and pedaled <u>faster</u>.

19. <u>Oh, no!</u> The horse did <u>not</u> clear the fence, and the rider is down.

20. Gillian grabbed the bar and waited for the wind to tug her <u>hang</u> glider into open air.

SENTENCES

A. *Directions:* Write the subject(s) of each of the following sentences in the space provided at the end.
   EXAMPLE: The dragon devoured St. George. ____*dragon*____

   1. Maxwell drank every drop of his coffee. _____

   2. Yesterday Mr. Proctor gambled all his money and lost.

   _____

3. The crest of the wave swept Chauncey Colgate off his surfboard.

   _____

4. The king's favorite burgers came from the corner cafe.

   _____

5. On Monday the police found the janitor in a drum.

   _____

6. The scope of the investigation takes my breath away.

   _____

7. The powerful surf dragged the washing machine out with the tide. _____

8. My three sons did a fantastic job on the bathroom walls.

   _____

9. This morning Melvin and Bess pledged to wax the old table.

   _____

10. The dirty dishes cascaded to the floor. _____

11. The removal of the garbage bags made them all glad.

    _____

12. Did Rose really leave her cereal bowl on the post?

    _____

13. The Quakers next door raise hay and oats. _____

14. Peter skipped his peanut butter sandwich today.

    _____

15. Sal, Tad, and Fred drank their juice with the spray of the ocean in their faces. _____

16. The weather in Canada was dry all summer. _____

17. Morton likes lots of salt on his potatoes. _____

18. Why will there be no soup at Mrs. Campbell's wedding reception?

    _____

19. Every day Duncan eats four doughnuts for breakfast.

    _____

20. Scott sneezed and reached for another tissue.

    _____

B. *Directions:* In the space at the end of each group of words, write **F** if it is a fragment, **R** if it is a run-on, or **S** if it is a sentence.

EXAMPLE: Chuck ran to school. _S_

1. Singing all those songs again at the top of his lungs. _____
2. Even if we were going to the North Pole on a camel. _____
3. Mt. Rushmore is located in South Dakota. _____
4. Tunney won the poetry award, that's why he's smiling. _____
5. When the baby saw his mother. _____
6. Yes, I know exactly what I'm doing. _____
7. Tony sprained his ankle on the hike, it really hurt. _____
8. Meeting the governor after the banquet. _____
9. Driving at high speeds frightened Carter. _____
10. Gracie was nervous about the biology quiz. _____
11. Jake looked in the open window then he climbed inside. _____
12. In the middle of the night rushing through the tall trees. _____
13. Although she admitted she hadn't seen the circus before. _____
14. John Steinbeck wrote *The Grapes of Wrath.* _____
15. Scared that he would have to take his little brother. _____
16. We spent the day hiking my feet ached that night. _____
17. Manuel left the house that morning, consequently, he missed the fire. _____
18. Into the lake, feeling the cold water on his shoulders. _____
19. The Russian serfs were freed in 1863. _____
20. Since Rita ran in the marathon, this past summer. _____

C. *Directions:* Revise the following groups of words into one *or* two complete sentences. You may have to add words, capitalize letters, or change or insert punctuation.

EXAMPLE: He sat down she sat down next to him
      He sat down. She sat down next to him.

1. On the top of the refrigerator in the kitchen

   _____

2. Hank played the guitar his sister played the fiddle

   _____

3. If Beth wins the lottery tonight

   _____

4. The wailing of the ambulance's siren

   _____

5. Ted watched television for eight hours his brain turned to mush

_____

6. Julie eyed the shark with suspicion then she decided to leave the water

_____

7. Spinning on top of the table

_____

8. Bilbo Baggins is the hero of *The Hobbit* it is a wonderful book

_____

9. After Professor Blake finished his brilliant lecture

_____

10. Over the fence and through the field the horse

_____

11. Why are you going home, I said I'm sorry

_____

12. When Shoji saw the pumpkins covered with frost

_____

13. Henry James was a novelist, William James was a philosopher

_____

14. During the hurricane many of the houses

_____

15. Rudyard Kipling was born in India then he went to school in England

_____

D. *Directions:* Depending on what type of sentence it is, write *simple* or *compound* in the space after each of the following sentences.
EXAMPLE: Biff loves spaghetti. _____ *simple* _____

1. Jamila won the race, but she collapsed at the finish line. _____

2. The sailor saw the lighthouse flash again. _____

3. Len bought the coat and paid in cash. _____

4. The Germans won some battles, yet they lost the war.

_____

5. Betsy missed first base, so the umpire called her out.

_____

6. Andres and Nancy saw a flying saucer. _____

7. Thirty penguins escaped from the aquarium.

   _____

8. They talked and laughed on the way to the zoo.

   _____

9. No, I don't like fried squid. _____

10. The U.S. calls them astronauts, but the U.S.S.R. calls them cosmonauts. _____

11. Either you apologize to your brother, or you stay in your room.

    _____

12. Sandy told a ghost story, and Andrea made the popcorn.

    _____

13. Fern is a wonderful gardener. _____

14. Sue and Sally asked Rico and Ron to the big dance.

    _____

15. Lorraine beats Bill at tennis, so she lets him win at checkers.

    _____

16. I love to get up early and read the paper by myself.

    _____

17. He walked to the edge of the cliff, and he looked down at the rocks. _____

18. George Eliot's real name was Mary Ann Evans.

    _____

19. Roberta saw a snake, and Albert caught a wild pig.

    _____

20. Would you like to eat dinner or go to the park?

    _____

PUNCTUATION

A. *Directions:* Insert the correct punctuation where it is needed in the following sentences. You may add *'s* when necessary.
   EXAMPLE: Heres your hat Tom
            Here's your hat, Tom.

   1. The two girls books floated away
   2. Cant you find the house either Myrtle
   3. Yes Im doing my homework Elsa said

4. Dont touch that poisonous lizard
5. Did you find Charles coat
6. Marie looked up and said I cant find the glue
7. Ed couldnt go on the weekend trip so Bomani cancelled it
8. Cheryl loves to eat shrimp scallops clams and lobster
9. Wouldnt you like to see the Smiths cat chase a mouse Fred
10. Oh Im afraid Ill have to skip the meeting tonight
11. To cousin Will Sam was a tremendous bore
12. Get out of my flowers
13. Antonio told us that his mothers cold was better
14. She said Im going to bed and went upstairs
15. Arent you going to watch the girls soccer team Kim asked
16. Martha picked up her brother brushed off his pants and sent him home
17. Ann isnt very friendly but shes not mean
18. In paragraph three above your name is mentioned
19. Why cant you ever wear red white and blue clothes Cornelius Amy inquired
20. The sheeps farmer lives in that small hut but he is rich

B. *Directions:* Rewrite the following sentences using correct punctuation marks.

EXAMPLE: Slim likes fish!

Slim likes fish.

1. Ann said "we should come to her house on Friday."

_____

2. "Are'nt you keeping score, Ed," I asked.

_____

3. Judy likes beef chicken, and, pork, but she hates lamb.

_____

4. Ouch. That shot really hurt doctor.

_____

5. Womens' clothes are more expensive than men's clothes.

_____

6. "I should'nt have come to dinner" Edward said sadly?

_____

7. Christine called her friend, and talked for three hours.

_____

8. Jane suddenly said "I've never read *Treasure Island*!

_____

9. Yes the Baxter's mouse died yesterday.

_____

10. "Robin Hood is a legendary hero,"the teacher, said.

_____

11. Holly said that "she would'nt want her mother to see her grades."

_____

12. Against Uncle Red Sam didn't have a chance?

_____

13. "Oh she doesn't know what shes talking about, Alice said coldly."

_____

14. Tony saw Mary's house and he gasped at it's size.

_____

15. "Her's is the best cider I've ever tasted." he said.

_____

ERRORS

A. *Directions:* Each of the following sentences contains at least one error. Find each error and circle it.

EXAMPLE: Have(n't) we seen this movie before(.)

1. At the store there is many kinds of fruit.
2. I accidently sent the postcard to Tucson Arizona
3. With her aunt Harriet went to the mountains.
4. John said that "he would like to buy the new album".
5. Tazume gave his present to Alan, and Molly gave her's to Jeff.
6. "Oh, no" said Jared. "I didn't feed the dog".
7. We arrived in Florence Italy by train on Monday July 21, 1986.
8. The class read "The Grapes of Wrath", a novel by John Steinbeck.
9. "Where are the coins " asked Hal?
10. Havent you put the books on the shelves and the chalk in the drawer yet.
11. Joshua was worried that the package wouldn't arrive on time but Mrs. Henry said that its on its way.
12. Marc asked, "when is sports classes meeting"?
13. Juliana decided to recite *Velvet shoes*, by Elinor Wylie, for the poetry contest.
14. Henry borrowed Janets notes because he had missed class on tuesday.
15. "Shoot I missed the last bus," wailed Lou. "now Ill have to walk two miles!"

16. Lydia packed her knapsack, canteen, sleeping, bag compass, and hiking boots for her hike in the Grand canyon.

17. The group of firefighters and their spouses are traveling to Cleveland for a convention.

18. In the American West not only the cowboys but also the farmers chased away the buffalo?

19. Emma didnt attend the assembly, and her teacher, Ms. Kaminsky called Emmas home.

20. In the local newspaper, "News of The Week", several meetings of the town council was announced.

B. *Directions:* Correct the error in each of the following sentences.

EXAMPLE: My mother gave her picture to my father, but Aunt Sue gave her(s) to me. *hers*

1. Whenever you go.
2. Several of that type is found in the drawer.
3. The bicycle was just the one I wanted but I didn't have enough money.
4. By Thursday Winifred still had'nt given Leroy the assignment for class.
5. We decided that the entire class will leave for Nova Scotia, Canada on Friday August 17, 1993.
6. "Wow! I can't believe the leaves have already changed color!" exclaimed Jim. "Its only the beginning of September."
7. Before you read any more of *Anne Of Green Gables*, take out the trash, dry the dishes, and feed the cat.
8. Marion had to decide immediately whether to sign the letter "Yours truely" or Sincerely yours."
9. After singing "Yankee Doodle," the children went outside Benjamin fell down on the playground and had to be treated by the nurse.
10. There were tables of children's toys and clothing, men's and womens' clothing, antiques, and collectibles.
11. I don't know whether I should leave immediately, or whether I should wait until the rain stops and perhaps be late?
12. If you keep this dog, you must give away, either your guppies or your boa constrictor.
13. "Where are the group of candidates for the election supposed to meet?" asked Ned noisily.
14. The mysterious stranger arrived and whined irritably, "Doesn't anyone remember my name?"
15. Just because I gave you the biggest piece of cake.
16. Leaving the party early, Mr. and Ms Hughes went to Burger Bites and ate the Super Chewy Veggie Burger with home fries.

17. The post card arrived wrinkled and grimy, and I could barely make out the picture of lake Silver Bow with Mount Camel's Hump in the background.

18. Yesterday I went to school to take my history test and then I went to my piano lesson.

19. Not only does the Jefferson High school Student Council want to hold a dance, but it will do whatever is necessary to convince the school administration.

20. On Tuesday either you or I are going to run the movie projector, for Ms. Wang will be out of town at a teacher's convention.